Emotional and Behavioral Problems in Children with Learning Disabilities

Emotional and Behavioral Problems in Children with Learning Disabilities

Robin P. Gallico, Ed.D.
Kennedy Institute
Special Education Department
Baltimore, Maryland

Thomas J. Burns, Ph.D.
Child and Adolescent Program
Howard County Mental Health Center
Columbia, Maryland
Private Practice
Baltimore, and Columbia, Maryland

Charles S. Grob, M.D.
University of California-Irvine Medical Center
Department of Psychiatry
Orange, California

A College-Hill Publication
Little, Brown and Company
Boston/Toronto/San Diego

College-Hill Press
A Division of
Little, Brown and Company (Inc.)
34 Beacon Street
Boston, Massachusetts 02108

Library of Congress Cataloging in Publication Data
Main entry under title:

Gallico, Robin P., 1948–
    Emotional and behavioral problems in children with
learning disabilities.
    "A College-Hill publication."
    Bibliography: p. 127.
    Includes index.
    1. Learning disabled children — Mental health.
2. Child psychiatry.   I. Burns, Thomas J., 1951–
II. Grob, Charles S., 1950–   .   II. Title.
[DNLM: 1. Affective Symptoms — etiology.   2. Affective
Symptoms — in infancy & childhood.   3. Child Behavior
Disorders — etiology.   4. Learning Disorders — complications.
WS 350.6 G168e]
RJ506.L4G35   1987   618.92'8588   87-26176

ISBN 0-316-30286-4

Printed in the United States of America

To:
Stephanie,
Rebecca,
Noah & Gabriel,
and in memory
of Ian

Contents

Appendices

Foreword

*T*he learning-disabled child rarely suffers from an isolated deficit in cognitive performance. Rather, clinical experience fortified by the results of epidemiologic studies indicates that the learning-disabled child often presents with a complex series of related problems affecting self-concept, peer interactions, family relationships, and, not infrequently, involvement with juvenile authorities. Accordingly, while the immediate problem for the learning-disabled child may be poor academic performance, the full evaluation and effective management of the child often crosses many disciplines, including education, psychology, psychiatry, and social work. Nevertheless, the ideal of the interdisciplinary evaluation and treatment of the learning-disabled child is prevented from becoming a reality all too frequently because of a number of barriers that prevent effective interdisciplinary approaches. The present volume, written by an educator, a psychologist, and a psychiatrist, who work together in a school within a clinical setting for learning-disabled children, makes a major contribution in clearly articulating what those barriers are, and in delineating strategies for effective cross-discipline communication and treatment to transcend these barriers.

A fundamental problem, eloquently discussed by Dr. Gallico, centers on the rather rigid legal distinctions between *learning-disability* and *emotional disorder*, as defined by the entitlement laws. Thus, the diagnoses tend to be nearly mutually exclusive, whereas clinical experience and epidemiologic data indicate a very high prevalence of learning disability in emotionally disturbed children, as well as a high incidence of behavioral and emotional disorders in learning-disabled children. Needless to say, virtually all significant psychiatric disturbances in children will impair their ability to learn in a traditional classroom setting. As a consequence, approximately one-fifth of children requiring special educational services for learning problems are found to be suffering from primary emotional disturbance.

Another barrier to the effective evaluation process and provision of services is the differences in diagnostic nosology from the educational and psychiatric perspectives. Mental health workers generally present the diagnoses of emotionally disturbed children in format of the Diagnostic and Statistical Manual III (DSM-III). Since the diagnostic terminology of DSM-III may be foreign to educators, Dr. Grob provides a clear and succinct explanation of the multi-axial diagnostic classification and a description of the major diagnostic entities. It is noteworthy that Axis I of this diagnostic schema is restricted to clinical psychiatic syndromes, whereas Axis II contains the specific developmental disorders related to learning. A clear understanding of the conceptual and nosologic framework of the DSM-III will greatly aid educators in integrating information from psychiatric sources into the complete evaluation of the learning-disabled child with behavioral problems, or the emotionally disturbed child.

The etiologic relationships between behavioral disturbances and learning disorders remain poorly understood. As reviewed by Dr. Burns, psychological studies suggest that the demoralization associated with academic failure and specific problems with social interactions due to communicational difficulties may contribute to the high prevalence of behavioral and emotional disorders among these children. Furthermore, observing the frustration of their parents resulting from these disorders may prove an additional burden for the children to carry during developmental life experience. Clearly, these and related issues must be addressed in the psychotherapeutic treatment of the symptomatic child.

Nevertheless, correlation does not prove causality, and *post hoc, propter hoc* errors of logic must be avoided. Findings emerging from behavioral neuroscience now provide evidence that neuronal systems involved in memory may also affect attention, mood, and arousal state. Thus, there may be reason for considering that the high association of certain behavioral problems, such as attention deficit disorder with hyperactivity, with learning disorders represents dysfunction in common neuronal systems. Furthermore, human genetics study is providing evidence that certain types of learning disorders, behavioral disorders, and psychiatric disorders exhibit a Mendelian pattern of inheritance. Such studies may not only shed light on etiology, but also point to complicating factors within families where both the parent and child suffer from a significant learning, communicational, or psychiatric disorder that may further disrupt the parent–child relationship.

As demonstrated in this book through example cases, an effective treatment plan that addresses both the cognitive as well as the emotional symptoms in learning disabilities requires an interdisciplinary approach. However, it is only through an informed appreciation of the different disciplinary perspectives, their diagnostic terminology and their treatment strategies, that a coherent management plan can be developed that adequately deals with the complex and interrelated cognitive, psychological, and neuropsychiatric aspects of the learning-disabled child. It is hoped that this book will serve as a road map to guide the concerned educator and pediatric mental health professional through this complex and difficult terrain so that they may optimize services for the learning-impaired child.

Joseph T. Coyle, M.D.
Distinguished Service Professor of Child Psychiatry
Director, Division of Child Psychiatry
Professor of Psychiatry, Neuroscience, Pharmacology
    and Pediatrics
The Johns Hopkins Hospital and School of Medicine

Acknowledgments

The authors would like to acknowledge the staff and students of the Kennedy Institute School in Baltimore, Maryland for their unending support and source of information. Additional thanks are due Dr. Michael Bender for his continuous encouragement throughout this project.

Preface

*T*he interrelatonship between learning disabilities and emotional disturbance has recently received increasing attention by researchers and educators alike. Much of this attention has focused on the deficient social skills of learning-disabled students, but recommendations for possible intervention strategies are not plentiful.

Emotional and Behavioral Problems in Children with Learning Disabilities is designed to address the many facets of this relationship: theory, research, application, and direct service. Its intended audience is teachers, both special and general education, and all mental health professionals who work with teachers on a regular basis. The book bridges the disciplines of education, medicine, and psychology, and explains in understandable terms the language of each discipline. In this way, educators, psychologists, and physicians can better communicate in the cooperative manner mandated by Public Law 94-142.

This text is arranged in three major sections that address the facts, questions, and issues regarding the nature of learning disabilities, the similarities and differences between learning disabilities and emotional disorders, and the procedures currently used to measure and treat each of these disabilities. Section I provides an educational and social perspective. Chapters 1 and 2 introduce the reader to the similarities and differences between learning disabilities and emotional disturbance and review current research relating the two. The focus of Chapter 3 on peer and family relations provides a discussion of the social functioning of learning-disabled students, while highlighting potential risk factors and social disabilities.

Section II, The Medical and Psychiatric Perspective, is comprised of two chapters designed to explain to educators psychiatric diagnosis using the medical profession's classification system and to review current management of some disorders through medication. The charts in Chapter 5 were developed as a quick reference guide to use of medications.

Finally, Section III addresses the treatment perspective with a focus on approaches to psychosocial treatment, and on coordination of services to the child and family.

Case studies have been provided as a means of demonstrating how theory, diagnosis and treatment actually apply to individuals within a school setting. These experiences have been drawn from over a decade of working in a clinical school setting. It has been the experience of the authors that the supposedly clear boundaries between disability categories such as learning disabilities and emotional disturbance become confused and overlap as the severity of each disorder increases. In light of the current emphasis in education on cross categorical grouping and mainstreaming, it is our belief that teachers must be adequately prepared to address both these disability groups with equal competence. It is our hope that this book will aid toward this goal.

An Educational and Social Perspective

The Social, Emotional, and Behavioral Problems of Learning Disabilities

*T*eachers of learning-disabled students are often faced with a range of secondary emotional problems which manifest themselves in disruptive behavior in the classroom. Years of frustration over academic failure and unsatisfactory peer relationships may lead to a poor attitude about school. The situation often results in a see-saw effect with learning disabilities on one end and emotional problems on the other. The teacher then is faced with a balancing act with one side or the other weighing more heavily on the student's school performance. There are times when more attention is given to remediation of academic deficits, and traditionally, learning-disability programs have been successful in this area. However, there are also times when a student's emotional state needs greater attention, and in this realm, learning-disability teachers are often underprepared.

A relationship between learning disabilities and emotional and behavioral problems has been established in epidemiological surveys such as The Isle of Wight and London studies (Rutter, 1970; Rutter & Yule, 1974; Sturge, 1982). These studies found a significant relation-

3

ship between reading retardation (or reading disability) and conduct disorders. This type of student, one who is a virtual nonreader and is evidencing delinquent behavior, is at risk for dropping out of school and becoming a burden on the social and legal system. Other clinical research (Forness, Bennett, & Tose, 1983; Stone & Rowley, 1964; Tamkin, 1960) has highlighted a full spectrum of learning problems in students with emotional disturbance that extends beyond reading into all academic areas. These academic deficits have been shown to contribute to poor school adjustment.

Recent attempts to broaden our understanding of how children with learning disabilities function have focused on these students' poor self-esteem and behavior problems that accompany their academic deficits (Cullinan, Epstein, & Dembinski, 1979; Epstein, Cullinan, & Rosemier, 1983). Many attempts have been made to differentiate the categories of learning disabilities and emotional disturbance using test profiles and other diagnostic information with minimal success (Becker, 1978; Chandler & Jones, 1983a, 1983b; McCarthy & Paraskevopoulos, 1969). Professionals continue to debate the best method for grouping handicapped students. Some would argue that it is more beneficial to group special education students according to the type and severity of their handicap. In light of the current controversy over the efficacy of categorical versus noncategorical class groupings (Carlberg & Kavale, 1980; Gajar 1980; Phipps, 1982; Ysseldyke & Algozzine, 1982), it is important to examine the interaction of learning disabilities and behavior. Consider the case of John:

Case Study #1: Learning Disability or Emotional Disturbance?

John was an 8 year old boy whose previous school history was significant for multiple disciplinary removals. Intelligence testing revealed a youngster with significant language disability as well as a serious articulation disorder. However, John's nonverbal intelligence, his understanding of spatial relations, for example, was in the superior range. As expected, John's academic performance was at the readiness level at best — that is, when he would cooperate at all with the demands of testing.

John had a very close relationship with his mother and she often acted protectively, jumping to his defense and rescuing him from the frustrations of school. Consequently, John preferred the safe harbor of "home and mother" to the more stormy conditions at school. John's extreme anxiety in school resulted in his frequent flight out of the classroom, usually in an angry huff, his wandering aimlessly around the room, or in his destruction of academic papers (his and others). John was so terrified of failure that he insisted on manipulating and controlling every encounter with his teachers. If his teacher gave him five problems, he would only do two. If 10 minutes of work was required to earn a star, John would negotiate for five minutes. This constant bargaining behavior wore his teachers down to the point of total frustration. John could not accept any limit imposed by an authority figure. John could not quietly take a "time out" from frustrating situations. When his teachers were forced to physically remove him, his panic resulted in his hitting, spitting, biting, and scratching. However, if his teacher devoted her full one-to-one attention to John, allowing him to control the learning activity, he demonstrated the ability to succeed.

WHO IS LEARNING DISABLED? WHO IS EMOTIONALLY DISTURBED?

It is difficult to identify clearcut guidelines that would clarify the nature of either learning disabilities or emotional disturbance. Results pertaining to the distinctness of these disabilities are inconclusive and attempts to measure similarities and differences in these two groups have been fraught with difficulties.

Public Law 94-142 has separate definitions for both categories and requires that educational teams distinguish between learning disability and serious emotional disturbance by assigning a primary handicapping condition. This is done partly to satisfy the federal government's regulations for reporting the number of children served in each category to determine the amount of financial assistance given to each state. This information, however, is then also used to assign students to programs or classrooms equipped to deal with specific special education needs. Such important decisions as these are often made without consideration of the full range of complex questions involved in the diagnosis, assessment, and differentiation of learning disability and emotional disturbance. In fact, the P.L. 94-142 definitions of learning disability and emotional disturbance contain exclusionary factors that must be ruled out before a diagnosis can be made. It is assumed, then, that these groups of children are so different that such a distinction is possible, and that cognitive, perceptual, psycholinguistic, and social behaviors vary significantly between the learning-disabled and the emotionally disturbed child. Current practices can best be highlighted by examining the federal definitions and issues relating to measurement for both categories. As will be demonstrated, both definitions have common elements, such as reference to academic problems, and exclusionary clauses which make their coexistence impossible.

DEFINITION OF LEARNING DISABILITY

The definition of learning disability is exclusionary in nature. That is, it specifies what etiological factors must be ruled out to determine its existence. The definition does not clearly explain what specific factors actually contribute to its existence.

Federal Definition

Public Law 94-142 defines learning disability as

a disorder in one or more of the basic psychological processes involved in the understanding or in using language, spoken or written, which may manifest itself in an imperfect ability to listen, think, speak, read, write, spell, or to do mathematical calculations. The term includes such conditions as perceptual handicaps, brain injury, minimal brain dysfunction, dyslexia, and developmental aphasia. The term does not apply to children who have learning problems which are primarily the result of visual, hearing, or motor handicaps, of mental retardation, of emotional disturbance, or of environmental, cultural or economic disadvantage. (P.L. 94-142, Part B 34 C.F.R. 300.5 (b) (9))

Measurement Issues

The most common procedure for determining the existence of an inability to learn that is caused by a specific learning disability is to demonstrate a severe ability-achievement discrepancy. The regulations and procedures for evaluating specific learning disabilities (U.S. Office of Education, 1977) provide only vague references to team decisions and the existence of a severe discrepancy between achievement level and intellectual ability. The 1984 report of the United States Department of Education, Special Education Programs Work Group on Measurement Issues in the Assessment of Learning Disabilities (Reynolds, et al, 1985a) has now offered recommended procedures for determining discrepancies. Unfortunately, these recommendations have been slow to filter down to the school team level. Thus, educators have relied upon qualified examiners, most often psychologists, to sort out the answers and to verify the existence of a severe discrepancy. This has traditionally been done in one of four ways: (1) number of years of academic achievement below grade level,

(2) ability-achievement discrepancy score, (3) WISC-R verbal perform-ance discrepancy, and (4) WISC-R profile analysis (see review by Berk, 1984). Recent work in discrepancy calculation, however, has seriously questioned the reliability and validity of most available methods (Berk, 1982, 1983, 1984; Kaufman, 1976a, 1976b; Reynolds et al, 1985; Vance, Singer, Kitson, & Brenner, 1983; Ysseldyke, Algozzine, & Epps, 1983). This suggests that further refinement is needed in both the federal definition and the diagnistic procedures used to measure learn-ing disability. Ysseldyke and Algozzine (1982) pointed out that research has failed to identify those characteristics that are universal and specific to learning disabilities. Certainly, underachievement is universal, but it is not specific only to the learning disabled. McLeod (1983) summarized the definition versus diagnosis problems:

> Attempts to define learning disability have been bedeviled by confusing definition with diagnosis, by trying to reconcile dis-parate views from different vested interest groups, and by react-ing irrationally to the concept of discrepancy between actual and expected achievement. (p. 20)

Because the federal definition is so vague, that is, defining learning disability by excluding other possible causes, individual states develop their own criteria or the states allow school systems to do it. Conse-quently, differing child counts for learning disability exist among states and within states.

DEFINITION OF EMOTIONAL DISTURBANCE

The definition of emotional disturbance also contains exclusion-ary phrases and references to learning problems. It states that intellec-tual, sensory, and health factors can not be the cause of the academ-ic problem.

Federal Definition

Public Law 94-142 defines serious emotional disturbance as a

> condition exhibiting one or more of the following characteristics over a long period of time and to a marked degree, which adversely affects educational performance:
> a. an inability to learn which cannot be explained by intellectual, sensory or health factors;
> b. an inability to build or maintain satisfactory interpersonal relationships with peers and teachers;

c. inappropriate types of behavior or feelings under normal circumstances;

d. a general pervasive mood of unhappiness or depression; or

e. a tendency to develop physical symptoms or fear associated with personal or school problems.

The term includes children who are schizophrenic. The term does not
include children who are socially maladjusted, unless it is determined that
they are also seriously emotionally disturbed. (P.L. 94-142, Part B 34 C.F.R.
300.5 (b) (8))

In an often-quoted article on the future of special education for
emotionally disturbed children, Kaufman (1980) summarized the
current status of problems with the definition of emotional disturbance. He went on to say,

> How is one to reconcile a definition that says if a child fails to
> develop satisfactory relations with peers and adults or exhibits
> one or more of the other four characteristics to a marked extent
> and over a period of time then he or she is disturbed, with an
> exclusionary clause which says that a child can be socially mal-
> adjusted but not disturbed? That is the kind of ambiguity of
> language and frailty of logic that keeps lawyers busy and drives
> decent people insane. The fact is that there is no clear, unambig-
> uous definition of emotional disturbance. (p. 524)

Measurement Issues

Basic to the category of emotional disturbance is the inability to
learn. Bower & Lambert (1965) felt that this inability to learn was the
single most significant characteristic of the emotionally handicapped
student. The fact that separate categories of learning disability and
emotional disturbance exist assumes that it should be possible to
determine accurately the difference between a disorder in a basic psychological process (learning disability) and an inability to learn due to
emotional disturbance. The studies to be reviewed in Chapter 2 of this
book do not support this assumption. In fact, these two categories are
more alike than they are different. Caution must be taken not to
assume that an inability to learn is synonymous with academic deficits. Any child who is unable to function in a traditional classroom
because he or she is behaving aggressively, or withdrawing excessively,
or whose attentions are diverted away from learning because of anxiety, is clearly not learning up to potential.

Relying on test scores alone often results in a narrow interpretation and may result in a misclassification of a handicapping condition.

It is important to note that test scores will demonstrate the inability to learn, but will not identify the reason for this failure to achieve.

DEFINITION BY MEDICAL AND HEALTH PROFESSIONALS

The medical profession, often relied on for its expertise in emotional disorders, does not use the P.L. 94-142 definitions of learning disability and emotional disturbance. Rather, it has developed its own diagnostic manual, the *Diagnostic and Statistical Manual III* (DSM-III), which provides for multiaxial (to be defined in Chapter 4) diagnostic criteria utilized by the major mental health professionals (American Psychiatric Association, 1983). This diagnostic manual and its set of criteria will be discussed in some length in Section II. There have been few attempts to match the psychiatric DMS-III manual with educational language and definitions (Foreness & Cantwell, 1980).

Cooperation between special education and other mental health professionals can only be achieved through a systematic effort to understand each other's professional frame of reference (Forness & Cantwell, 1982). By understanding the DSM-III, it may be easier for school personnel to relate psychiatric assessments and mental health consultations to educational team decision making. Often, school teams misinterpret psychiatric reports utilizing the DSM-III multiaxial diagnosis because they contain a different language and omit the specific term *serious emotional disturbance.* In a broad sense, the DSM-III (1983) defines mental disorder by excluding social deviancy:

> In DSM-III each of the mental disorders is conceptualized as a clinically significant behavioral or psychological syndrome or pattern that occurs in an individual and that is typically associated with either a painful symptom (distress) or impairment in one or more important areas of functioning (disability). In addition, there is an inference that there is a behavioral, psychological, or biological dysfunction, and that the disturbance is not only in the relationship between the individual and society. (p. 6)

When the disturbance is limited to a conflict between an individual and society, it may represent social deviance, but is not by itself a mental disorder. The difficulties in making this differentiation between social deviancy (social maladjustment in P.L. 94-142 language) and emotional disturbance appears to leave open to interpretation such questions as whether a child is disturbed or socially maladjusted.

Educational teams have relied on clinical or school psychologists or psychiatrists as qualified examiners to determine whether a child is seriously emotionally disturbed. A comprehensive evaluation of a student should cover many domains and should include some measure of ability, achievement, behavioral and social adaptive functioning, classroom observations, and an objective measure of emotional adjustment usually achieved through a clinical interview and projective testing.

NUMBER OF CHILDREN SERVED

The Eighth Annual Report to Congress of The Education of the Handicapped Act, 1985, reports the most recent figures of numbers of handicapped children served (for the 1984–85 school year) furnished by the U.S. Office of Special Education Programs. This report indicated that 1,839,292 learning-disabled and 373,207 emotionally disturbed children were served under P.L. 94-142. The learning disability category represented 42 percent of all handicapped children served, as compared to 8 percent for the emotionally disturbed group.

Despite these national estimates, there is considerable variability in the incidence rates reported state by state. For instance, the state of Maryland served approximately 47,000 (52 percent) learning-disabled students and 4,100 (4 percent) emotionally disturbed students, while New York served 131,000 (45 percent) learning-disabled students and 45,000 (2 percent) emotionally disturbed students. In North Dakota, 5,100 (43 percent) learning-disabled students and 389 (3 percent) emotinally disturbed students were served. Although these figures certainly reflect population differences in the states, that alone cannot account for the state-to-state variability currently found in the base rates of these handicapping conditions (Table 1–1).

CHARACTERISTICS OF LEARNING DISABILITIES AND EMOTIONAL DISTURBANCE

Similarities and Differences

The P.L. 94-142 definition of serious emotional disturbance contains specific references to behaviors manifested, poor interpersonal relationships, immaturity, inappropriate behavior, unhappiness, and physical symptoms associated with personal or school problems. The definition does not define social maladjustment, but makes ruling it out primary to the classification of serious emotional disturbance. Many of these characteristics can be measured through the use of

TABLE 1-1.
Number and Percent of Handicapped Children Served by Special Education Category for the State of Maryland

	Learning Disability		Emotional Disturbance	
Jurisdiction	Number	Percent	Number	Percent
Baltimore	10,346	55.0	581	3.0
Harford County	1,583	45.0	54	1.6
St. Mary's County	647	32.5	64	3.2

Information taken from Office of Special Education Eighth Annual Report to Congress on the Implementation of P.L. 94-142.

behavior checkslists. These characteristics, although not unique to emotionally disturbed children, exist in greater frequency and severity in emotionally disturbed students than in the learning-disabled, mentally retarded, or normal populations. Cullinan, Epstein, and Lloyd (1983) summarized the research in this area as follows:

All three groups of handicapped students showed more extreme levels of Personality Problem than normals but did not significantly differ among themselves. On the Conduct Disorder factor, however, the behavior disordered pupils were much more extreme than normals, learning disabled, or mentally retarded. (p. 126)

Academic Deficits in Emotionally Disturbed Students

There is a relationship between academic deficit and emotional disturbance; however, even when certain variables are controlled and sound achievement measures are used, the extent and nature of those academic deficits remain unclear.

Early research (Stone & Rowley, 1964; Tamkin, 1960) found that between 30 and 60 percent of emotionally disturbed students demonstrated some degree of educational disability. These studies focused on reading and arithmetic and concluded that a greater deficiency existed in arithmetic in emotionally disturbed students. More recent research (Gallico, 1985; Glavin & Annesley, 1971; Glavin, Quay, & Werry, 1971) examined a broader range of academic abilities in separate subgroups of disturbed students and found significant underachievement. These studies will be examined in greater detail in Chapter 2 of this book.

Behavior Problems of Learning-Disabled Students

Learning-disabled students have been described as impulsive, distractible, experiencing perceptual difficulties, and having emotionally unsatisfying, stressful relationships with peers and adults because they lack necessary and basic age-appropriate interpersonal skills (Bryan, 1982; Bryan & Bryan, 1978; Werner, Bryan, & Pearl, 1981). Although recent research has focused on the social skills of the learning disabled, few studies have attempted to categorize and describe the behavior problems of these learning-disabled students. Studies that have attempted to do so have shown a similar pattern in these behavior problems, as has been found in the emotionally disturbed population, with the main difference occuring in the frequency and severity of the problems (Cullinan et al., 1979; Epstein, Cullinan, & Rosemier, 1983; Grieger & Richards, 1976; Harris, King, Reifler, & Rosenberg, 1984).

Researchers in the field have hypothesized that the severity of behavior problems will discriminate emotionally disturbed students from other handicapped students (Cullinan et al., 1979; Grieger & Richards, 1976; McCarthy & Paraskevopoulos, 1969). But, recent work by Gallico (1985) pointed out that as the severity of the academic disability increases, the range of discriminating behavior problems narrows. Thus, some learning-disabled students are quite similar in behavioral profile to some emotionally disturbed students.

Differentating Learning Disabilities from Emotional Disturbance

The diagnostic label assigned to an individual student often determines the type of educational intervention provided. The doctrine of least restrictive environment or mainstreaming, mandated by P.L. 94-142, has resulted in cross-categorical placement. That is, more often than not, midly handicapped students in many special education categories are being grouped together for instruction. The teacher then must have a broad range of expertise in teaching learning-disabled, emotionally disturbed, and mentally retarded students. When handicapped students with different disabilities are grouped, the outcomes, in terms of teacher effectiveness, student performance, and students' self concepts, result in frustration for both teachers and students. This has been true even when the students are in a self-contained classroom without nonhandicapped peers. Therefore, the question of categorical (i.e., classes for the learning disabled) versus noncategorical (i.e., classes for the mildly educationally handicaped) grouping remains unresolved partly because of the varying opinions on the ability to differentiate one group from another. In reviewing these issues as they relate to emotionally disturbed and learning-disabled students, several points emerge:

1. Considerable overlap exists in the teacher perceptions of behavior problems of learning-disabled and emotionally disturbed students.

2. Although learning-disabled students have behavior problems, emotionally disturbed students have more severe behavior problems.

3. Educational diagnostic test patterns have failed to differentiate the learning-disabled student from the emotionally disturbed student.

4. Intelligence test patterns such as the WISC-R profile analysis have failed to differentiate the learning-disabled student from the emotionally disturbed student.

Predicting Group Membership

Webster and Schenck (1977) looked at the poor predictive validity of the commonly used diagnostic measures and concluded that if a child was of average ability and functioning below grade level on reading achievement measures, the tendency was to label the child "learning disabled"; if the child's overall intelligence fell at the borderline/dull normal range and word analysis skills were at a level commensurate with borderline ability, the child was most likely labeled "mildly retarded"; if the student was of average ability and was performing close to grade level in reading, yet was still having problems learning, the child was classified "emotionally disturbed." Friedrich, Fuller, and Davis (1984) examined the "hit rate" (ability to correctly predict), using criteria established by a Michigan task force for differentating learning disability from emotional disturbance. They found it to be only .35 for grades 10 to 12 and .60 for grades 7 to 9.

Issues Relating to the Degree of Difference in Achievement, Frequency and Severity of Behavior Problems, and Measurement

Studies have compared ability and achievement and have attempted to document these academic deficits in a broad range of students with emotional and behavioral disorders (Calhoun & Elliott, 1977; Forness et al., 1983; Forness, Sinclair, & Russell, 1984; Glavin, 1974; Tamkin, 1960). Some studies have indicated that emotionally disturbed students have more deficiencies in spelling and reading, whereas others point to mathematics as the main area of deficit. In contrast, other studies have found that no academic deficiencies exist in emotionally disturbed students. Research by Bryan (1982) has suggested that parents and teachers view learning-disabled students differently than normal students, but, to date, there have been few in-depth studies of adjustment factors that describe the extent of emotional and behavioral problems in learning-disabled students. For the studies that have been completed, the results suggest that there are two broad dimensions of behavioral difficulty: conduct problems (acting out, aggression) and personality problems (anxiety, withdrawal, social deficiency). These problems are also present in the emotionally disturbed population, and the frequency and severity of these problems seem to distinguish the emotionally disturbed group from the learning-disabled group.

SUMMARY

Many factors contribute to the difficulty in differentating learning disability from emotional disturbance. Since there is great variability in the terminology and criteria used to classify students, assumptions regarding the generalizability and applicability of research results are not possible. In addition, technically inadequate measures have been used inappropriately to draw conclusions about the achievement levels of learning-disabled and emotionally disturbed students. Berk (1984) detailed the incorrect comparison of grade-equivalent scores to age-based IQ to determine ability-achievement discrepancy. These inadequacies in analytical techniques, individually or collectively, tend to produce erroneous results. If clinical professionals working in the field cannot agree on how to determine learning disabilities, how can teachers be expected to differentiate a learning problem from an emotional problem? This presents a challenge to our institutions of higher education as they design teacher competencies and prepare teachers for the role and responsibilities they will assume.

Research Relating Learning Disabilities and Emotional Problems

*T*he dilemma of diagnosis and classification of emotionally disturbed and learning-disabled students continues to plague school-based decision-making teams. In the past, research has generally focused on describing the characteristics of a single group of special education students rather than looking at similarities and differences across different groups of handicapped students. Although it is common in some states to place diagnostically different students in the same special classes, there have been few attempts, from a research perspective, to study these students cross-categorically.

A cross-categorical perspective is important, however, if we are to train teachers to effectively deal with a full range of learning and behavior problems which adversely effect a student's classroom performance. In addition, many special education classes already have a cross-section or variety of handicapped students grouped together. In light of this, special education professionals must address certain key questions:

1. Do emotionally disturbed and learning-disabled students have enough characteristics in common to justify grouping these students together for instructional purposes or are they so different as to require unique approaches for each group?

2. Can individual counseling and/or therapy and behavioral approaches used in emotionally disturbed classes be used effectively with learning-disabled students?

3. Is an ability-achievement discrepancy unique to learning-disabled students, or is there significant discrepancy in other disability groups?

4. Are the multisensory remedial techniques commonly used with learning-disabled students applicable to other underachieving students?

For the purpose of this chapter's review, studies examining the cognitive, achievement, and behavioral characteristics of learning-disabled and emotionally disturbed students will be organized into three main categories: (1) similarities and differences of learning-disabled and emotionally disturbed students, (2) academic problems of emotionally disturbed students, and (3) behavioral problems of learning-disabled students. The studies are presented in a chart format with a brief introduction preceding the chart and a summary at the end of the chapter.

SIMILARITIES AND DIFFERENCES OF EMOTIONALLY DISTURBED AND LEARNING-DISABLED STUDENTS

The question of how similar or different emotionally disturbed or learning-disabled groups of students are has been examined by many researchers. In reviewing these studies as a group, there is overwhelming evidence that learning-disabled and emotionally disturbed students have more similarities than differences. Most of the studies reviewed here concentrate on the relationship of learning and conduct problems (Table 2–1).

ACADEMIC PROBLEMS OF EMOTIONALLY DISTURBED STUDENTS

Studies that have examined the extent of academic deficits in emotionally disturbed students have reported conflicting degrees of low achievement and have focused on a limited range of academic skills. Some studies have found deficits mainly in reading and arithmetic skills, with arithmetic deficits greater than reading deficits. In contrast, some studies have found no deficits at all (Table 2–2).

BEHAVIOR PROBLEMS OF LEARNING-DISABLED STUDENTS

Few studies have focused solely on the behavior problems of learning-disabled students. Emphasis has been on examining the social interactions of these students without describing the specific behavior problems that are characteristic of the learning disabled. Certainly, the most common features of behavioral disturbance reported are those of overactivity, impulsivity, and distractability. (Behaviors that are characteristic of attention deficit disorder will be discussed in detail in Chapter 4). These behaviors, although secondary to the learning problems, create conflicts for the student within the classroom setting that need specific interventions (Table 2–3).

SUMMARY

In reviewing the various studies that have focused on learning-disabled and emotionally disturbed students, many problems, as well as important implications, can be identified.

Problems and Implications Regarding Academic Deficits

It may not be possible to differentiate underachievement that is the result of a process disorder (i.e., learning disability) from underachievement resulting from an emotional disturbance. Although this may present a challenging and interesting diagnostic dilemma, it should not cloud the issue regarding the need for specific remediation with these students.

Since conflicting degrees of educational disability have been reported for emotionally disturbed students, it is important that an in-depth educational evaluation be completed and that a prescription for remediating academic deficits be given the same consideration as planning the therapeutic intervention.

Diagnosticians must advocate more universally accepted criteria for assessing these students so that the best decisions can be made regarding placement. Severe ability-achievement discrepancies are likely to exist in emotionally disturbed as well as learning-disabled students. These students are more similar than different in terms of academic problems. This is particularly relevant when the numbers of students in each category being served nationwide is compared. Because there are more identified learning-disabled students, fewer appropriate special education services are available to emotionally disturbed students. In order to serve both groups of students more appro-

(text continued on page 36)

TABLE 2-1.

Similarities and Differences of Emotionally Disturbed and Learning-Disabled Students

Source	Subjects	Characteristics	Focus
McCarthy & Paraskevopoulos (1969)	36 LD (90% male) 100 ED (80% male) 41 average	Ages 5–15 IQ ranges: LD 71–123 ED 86–132 Grades 1.2–7.9	Observable social behaviors
O'Grady (1974)	30 LD 30 ED 30 normals	Ages 6–10 IQ ranges: LD 83–128 ED 85–138 Normals 79–143	Psycholinguistic abilities & socioeconomic status
Grieger & Richards (1976)	527 normals 28 ED & LD in primary placements 72 ED & LD in intermediate placements	IQs within average range	Behavior ratings

Tests Used	Methods	Results/Conclusion*
Behavior Problems Checklist (Quay & Peterson)	Factor analysis Two-way analysis of variance	1. High degree of similarity in ratings for LD and ED 2. Teachers perceived problems as differing in number &/or degree 3. ED rated differently on all 3 factors of conduct, personality & immaturity 4. LD rated differently on conduct *5. Conduct problems of restlessness, disruptiveness, attention seeking, fighting, irresponsibility, hyperactivity, & distractibility were most common
Stanford-Binet WISC Illinois Test of Psycholinguistic Abilities	Matched nomals to LD & ED for age, IQ and SES Stratified into 2 IQ and 3 SES Analysis of variance	1. Mean scores for LD & ED lower than for normals 2. LD & ED did not differ 3. Pattern of abilities not related to IQ 4. SES did show an effect on total abilities, favoring the advantaged on auditory-vocal & the disadvantaged on visual-motor *5. LD & ED equally deficient in overall psycholinguistic abilities, which were more dependent on IQ & SES than on diagnosis
Behavior Problems Checklist (Quay & Peterson)	Normal drawn from same schools Factor analysis Analysis of variance Frequency of students with problems Age-matched samples of equal size	1. Replicated earlier results on three dimensions: conduct, personality, immaturity 2. LD & ED higher than normals with boys higher than girls on conduct problems *3. Factors for LD & ED remarkably similar to normals, although more severe

(continued)

TABLE 2-1.

Similarities and Differences of ED and LD Students *(continued)*

Source	Subjects	Characteristics	Focus
Hallahan & Kaufman (1977)			Review of labels, categories, & behavior
Webster & Schenck (1977)	Case files of 1524 children labeled LD, EMR, ED, multihandicapped	Ages 6–17	Examination of diagnostic test patterns
Becker (1978)	20 severe LD/ED 20 mild LD 20 EMR	Ages 9–13 LD/ED mean IQ 98 LD mild mean IQ 83 EMR mean IQ 60	Noncategorical programming based on homogeneity and teacher training
Dean (1978)	60 LD 60 ED	Ages 6–4 to 13–6 LD identified using Chalfant & Schefflin's criteria ED conduct disorders but no specific learning problems	Differentiating by WISC-R profile analysis

Tests Used	Methods	Results/Conclusion*
	Review existing research	1. LD, mild retardation, & ED have a lot in common 2. Significant behavioral characteristics (IQ, achievement, personality) may not be associated with specific category *3. Reserach needed to validate use of IQ, personality, & underachievement as major criteria for grouping
WISC-R, WRAT	Discriminant analysis Factor analysis	1. Analysis consistently failed to discriminate LD from other groups *2. These tests have little utility in discriminating LD from other handicaps
WISC (digit span) Raven Progressive Matrices Matching Familiar Figures Test Puzzle Task Rod and Frame Test	Students randomly selected from special classes matched for age, mental age, & analysis of variance	1. EMR performed lower on problem-solving tasks *2. Assumptions regarding overlapping teacher competencies are questionable
WISC-R	Subjects matched for age, sex, grade placement, & SES t-test for independent samples multivariate analysis Stepwise discriminant analysis	1. ED performance IQ > verbal IQ; LD group did not differ in VIQ and PIQ 2. Differences in block design & object assembly favoring ED 3. Block design, vocabulary, picture arrangement & object assembly differentiated LD & ED profile *4. LD students had difficulty in perceptual organization while ED students displayed more verbal deficits

(continued)

TABLE 2–1.

Similarities and Differences of ED and LD Students *(continued)*

Source	Subjects	Characteristics	Focus
Gajar (1979)	122 ED 135 LD 121 EMR		Cross-categorical comparison on cognitive, affective, demographic characteristics
Cullinan, Epstein & Dembinski (1979)	172 LD 176 EMR 153 BD 309 nonhandicapped	Ages 6–18 All students in public schools	Comparison of behavior problems
Docherty & Culbertson (1982)	123 students originally classified in 1975 49 LD boys 30 ED boys 44 unclassified boys	Ages 10–15 LD & ED diagnosed by child study teams according to NJ law Attended public schools & two private schools	Follow-up of stability of classification
McKinney & Forman (1982)	20 EMR 20 matched normals 20 LD 20 matched normals 20 ED 20 matched normals 57 girls 63 boys	Ages 6–12 All students in resource and regular classes EMR IQs 50–70 LD ability-achievement discrepancy, mean IQ 90 ED history of behavior problems, mean IQ 87	Differentiation on the basis of behavior problems

Tests Used	Methods	Results/Conclusion*

WISC
WRAT reading,
  arithmetic, spelling
Behavioral Checklist
  (Quay & Peterson)
Demographic data on
  sex, race, SES
	Subjects randomly
	  selected from a pool
	Discrepancy based on
	  expected grade minus
	  actual level
		1. EMR overall cognitive level
		  below ED & LD but not in
		  achievement
		2. LD lower than ED in reading
		3. ED below LD & EMR in
		  arithmetic

Behavior Problem
  Checklist-Revised
	From pool 104 boys were
	  studied
	Split-plot factorial analysis
	  of variance using
	  category, age, &
	  dimension
		1. Significant differences
		  existed for category,
		  dimension, & category by
		  dimension but no difference
		  for age alone
		2. Categories best discriminated
		  from each other on basis of
		  conduct disorder &
		  personality rather than
		  maturity-immaturity

Follow-up using
  updated 3 year
  evaluation after
  initial classification
	Analysis using Chi square
	  & Wilkes Lambda
		1. Only questionable stability
		  existed
		2. 2 unclassified, 23% of LD &
		  60% of ED changed
		  classification
		*3. Classification status less
		  stable for LD & ED, with ED
		  being least stable

Classroom Behavior
  Inventory (Shaefer,
  Aaronson, &
  Edgerton)
WRAT reading
California Test of
  Basis Skills
	Multivariate analysis of
	  variance
	3 stepwise discriminant
	  function analyses
		1. No significant differences in
		  behavior for all 3 groups
		2. LD students rated more
		  favorably than EMR or ED
		3. LD perceived as more
		  independent and task
		  oriented
		4. ED perceived as more hostile
		  & less considerate
		5. EMR viewed as less
		  intelligent

(continued)

TABLE 2–1.

Similarities and Differences of ED and LD Students *(continued)*

Source	Subjects	Characteristics	Focus
McKinney & Forman (1982) *(continued)*		WRAT reading: EMR 70 LD 78 ED 84 CAT %ile: EMR 56 LD 41 ED 54	
Vance, Singer, Kitson, & Brenner (1983)			Profile analysis to differentiate LD & ED & nonhandicapped
Epstein & Cullinan (1983)	16 pairs of white, male behaviorally disordered & LD matched for age and IQ	Attended special classes in public schools	Comparison of academic performance
Chandler & Jones (1983a) (1983b)	LD & ED students	Undefined	LD or ED — Does it make any difference?
Harris, King, Reifler, & Rosenberg (1984)	30 LD & ED attending special schools matched for age	Ages 6–12	Comparision of behavior

Tests Used	Methods	Results/Conclusion*
		*6. Teachers can distinguish between groups when behavior is compared to typical nonhandicapped students
WISC-R	Review of previous research using WISC-R scatter analysis	1. Diagnosis of LD or ED cannot be made on basis of WISC-R alone 2. LD & ED cannot be differentiated on basis of psychological test results
WRAT Peabody Individual Achievement Test Gilmore Oral Reading Test	Grade equivalent scores used t-test computed on all pairs	1. BD students achieved higher scores in all cases 2. BD group near expected level in many areas whereas the LD group was not 3. Differences were in reading, reading rate, & language *4. Cross-categorical placement based on similarity of academic needs is not justified
None reported	Reviewed records	1. ED students routinely diagnosed as LD & served in resource rooms because of economic, administrative, pedagogical, social, & legal reasons 2. Problem lies in definition & diagnosis *3. ED children are programmed for exactly like LD
Child Behavior Checklist (Achenbach)	Rough guide used to determine grade level t-test for independent samples	1. No differences in amount of time in program or reading grade discrepancy score 2. LD scored higher on social competence

(continued)

TABLE 2-1.

Similarities and Differences of ED and LD Students *(continued)*

Source	Subjects	Characteristics	Focus
Harris, King, Reifler, & Rosenberg (1984) *(continued)*			
Cullinan & Epstein (1984)	360 public school children EMR, LD, BD, normal	Ages 5–20 EMR IQ 50–70 BD IQ above 70 & history of behavior problems LD IQ above 70 & severe under-achievement	Comparison of adjustment problems
Gallico (1985)	59 ED 40 LD	Ages 6–12.6 urban, low SES, attending special education nonpublic schools; diagnosed by school teams using Maryland state and federal guidelines	Application of a true score discrepancy method across LD & ED Compare groups in cognitive level, processing preference, ability-achievement discrepancy & behavior problems

LD = learning disabled; ED = emotionally disturbed; EMR = educable mentally retarded; BD = behavior disordered.

Tests Used	Methods	Results/Conclusion*
		3. ED scored higher on social withdrawal, self-destructive, inattentive, nervous/overactive
		*4. Profiles similar overall, but ED group more severe
Behavior Problem Checklist (Quay & Peterson)	Subjects matched across category & gender resulting in 15 groups of 8 matched pairs Split-plot factorial analysis of variance	1. Results replicated earlier dimensions of adjustment, conduct, & immaturity/ inadequacy
		2. BD group exceeded all others & LD group exceeded normals
		3. Pattern did not hold for senior high age
Kaufman Assessment Battery for Children Woodcock Johnson Psychoeducational Battery Child Behavior Checklist (Achenbach)	t-test for independent samples Chi Square analysis True Score difference method for calculating discrepancy Multivariate analyses for variance	1. No differences in overall cognitive ability, overall achievement, or overall behavior problems
		2. LD students were stronger in simultaneous processing skills
		3. LD students had significantly more severe discrepancies in all areas except reading comprehension & oral language
		4. Emotionally disturbed students behavior profiles revealed more internalizing behavior problems, i.e., self-destructive
		*5. ED & LD students who are severely disabled have more similarities in behavior & learning problems than differences

* These large-scale studies cannot easily be condensed; see original work for specific subject and method information.

TABLE 2-2.

Academic Problems of Emotionally Disturbed Students

Source	Subjects	Characteristics	Focus
Tamkin (1960)	34 children in residential treatment facility 22 boys 12 girls	Ages 8-7 to 9-4 All subjects hospialized IQs above 70	Survey of educational achievement
Stone & Rowley (1964)	116 students referred to a state facility for ED 82 boys 34 girls	Average age 12 IQ ranges 62-135	Replication of Tamkin's study
Motto & Lathan (1966)	47 students in a state psychiatric hospital 34 boys 13 girls	Ages 9-3 to 16-9 IQ 74-132	Achievement levels of students in state hospitals
Glavin & Annesley (1971)	Two categories: 34 conduct problems and 9 withdrawn children from three public schools	All males IQs above 70 All referred to a resource room	Correlates of conduct problems, withdrawal, reading, & arithmetic

Tests Used	Methods	Results/Conclusion*
WRAT — arithmetic and math	Set criteria for expected achievement based on chronological age Subtracted achievement rating from age	1. Average grade level was 3.8 for reading and 3.1 for math 2. Overall mean age appropriate for achievement 3. 32% did have educational disability & 41% were educationally advanced; 27% were at expected level *4. Educational disability not necessarily present in ED students
WRAT	Replicated Tamkin's procedures Repeated using mental age as basis for comparison	1. 60% fell into the disabled category, 21% in the expected category, & 20% in the advanced category 2. 52% were disabled, 19% expected, & 29% advanced 3. Lower scores found in arithmetic *4. Educational disability is closely associated with ED
California Achievement Tests	Used grade norms based on chronological age	1. No overall differences between reading & math achievement 2. Girls somewhat less deficient than boys 3. 43 out of 47 children below expectation in reading & math
Behavior Problems Checklist (Quay & Peterson) California Achievement Tests	Bond & Tinker's Formula for Discrepancy (IQ/100 × yrs. in school + 1) Classification into behavior categories Two tail t-test	1. 81.5% of behavior problem children underachieving in reading; 72.3% were underachieving in math 2. Majority fell into extreme underachievement 3. Higher achievement in arithmetic *4. Learning problems do not disappear after treatment of emotional problems

(continued)

TABLE 2-2.

Academic Problems of Emotionally Disturbed Students *(continued)*

Source	Subjects	Characteristics	Focus
Glavin, Quay, & Werry (1971)	Conduct problem children presenting severe difficulties in public school settings	Ages 7–6 to 11 IQs 89–112 50% black 50% white	2 year study of behavioral and academic gains of conduct problem children
Wright (1974)	47 boys drawn from 932 third graders rated by teachers as moderately to severely disruptive	Ages 7–10 to 10–3 IQs normal 26 whites 21 blacks	Percentage of students with behavior disorders demonstrating academic deficits
Rutter et al.† (1974)	Large number sample of 10 year old boys		Epidemiological studies of the Isle of Wight & an inner London borough

Tests Used	Methods	Results/Conclusion*
Behavior Problems Checklist (Quay & Peterson) California Achievement Test Wide Range Achievement Test	Students placed in controlled, experimental special classrooms Analysis of overt behavioral change	1. Academic gains & positive behavioral change more significant in the second year 2. Refuted belief that conduct problems must be changed before academic gain possible *3. A combination of academic remediation & behavioral intervention should occur simultaneously in a context of adequate behavioral control
California Short Form Test of Mental Maturity Graham-Kendall Memory for Design Wepman Auditory Discrimination Test Illinois Test of Psycholinguistic Abilities WISC Vocabulary Iowa Test of Basic Skills (reading comprehension)	Bond & Tinker's Reading Performance Index completed for each subject (IQ/100 × yrs. in school + 1) Product-moment correlation	1. 53% were underachieving in reading & another 17% were generalized underachievers 2. 29 of 47 had scores indicative of processing deficits; of the remaining boys, all but 1 had borderline deficits 3. Significant correlation between race & reading performance *4. Up to 51% of boys referred for conduct problems could have been identified as learning disabled
	Examined reading ability & four sets of variables: family discord, parental deviance, racial disadvantage, certain school characteristics	1. Reading retardation twice as common in 10 year old boys attending school in inner city London as on the rural Isle of Wight 2. All four variables found, but with greater frequency in urban environment

(continued)

TABLE 2–2.
Academic Problems of Emotionally Disturbed Students *(continued)*

Source	Subjects	Characteristics	Focus
Calhoun & Elliott (1977)	100 subjects 25 EMR in special class 25 ED in special class 50 (ED & EMR) on waiting list Randomly selected from 3 urban public schools	Students were either in special class or awaiting placement	Self concept, achievement, and mainstreaming
Sturge (1982)	From a pool of 1,689 10 year old boys 129 boys placed in 1 of 4 groups with or without reading &/or antisocial problems according to criteria (1) reading retarded (26 boys) (2) anitsocial (31 boys) (3) reading retarded & antisocial (39 boys) (4) control (33 boys)	All boys from an inner city borough of London	Follow-up to Isle of Wight Study Multifactorial causes of reading & conduct problems
Cantwell & Forness (1982)		editorial article	

Tests Used	Methods	Results/Conclusion*
Piers-Harris Children's Self-Concept Scale (Piers & Harris, 1969) Stanford Achievement Test	Data collected over a 3 year period Analysis of variance Teacher effectiveness controlled by rotating participating teachers	1. ED students in regular education had a more positive self-concept and higher achievement 2. Same held time for EMR students *3. Regular education & mainstreaming more effective than special classrooms
Reading Tests (National Foundation of Educational Research, U.K.), tests of nonverbal intelligence Teacher Rating of behavior (Rutter, 1967) Neale's Analysis of Reading Ability (1958) WISC (Subtests vocabulary, similarities, block design, object assembly)	Reading retardation defined as 2+ years behind, taking age & IQ into account by a regression formula (Rutter & Yule, 1975) Antisocial behavior defined by criteria score on rating measure Random selection of 112 boys with reading retardation Random selection of 159 boys with antisocial behavior Random selection of controls	1. 11% retarded in reading by more than 24 months while 17% had high antisocial ratings 2. Expectation of 2% having both reading & antisocial problems exceeded by close to twice (3.6%) 3. Poor concentration, motor restlessness, psychiatric contact by mother, & number of books in the home where factors found to differentiate retarded readers 4. Broken homes, family discord, history with police, probation or psychiatric contact by father, low socioeconomic status were factors differentiating antisocial boys
	Reviewed previous research	1. Anywhere from 0%–30% of a given sample of children referred to psychiatric facilities might be identified as learning disabled 2. A failure to account for IQ often leads to inaccurate conclusions regarding underachievement

(continued)

TABLE 2–2.

Academic Problems of Emotionally Disturbed Students *(continued)*

Source	Subjects	Characteristics	Focus
Cantwell & Forness (1982) *(continued)*			
Forness, Bennett, & Tose (1983)	92 children 23 girls 69 boys	Ages 7–12 IQs 67–133 82% white 10% black 5% Spanish 3% other Conduct disorder and anxiety disorders	Achievement of latency age ED students
Gallico (1985)	59 ED students 48 boys 11 girls	Ages 6 to 12–6 IQs 51–113 All students in special education schools for ED students All students from an urban setting	Academic deficits and learning disabilities of ED students

Tests Used	Methods	Results/Conclusion*
		*3. The relationship between learning disorders, especially reading disorders, to psychiatric disorders established by Rutter (1970) was considered
Peabody Individual Achievement Test WISC-R	Underachievement determined by subtracting level of achievement from expected grade level Division into 6 equally distributed age groups Adjusted achievement scores compared to samples from previous (1) severe (1+ yr behind) (2) moderate (½–1 yr behind) (3) minimal (less than ½ yr behind) Achievement adjusted for mental age	1. No significant differences were found between boys & girls 2. 10 year olds displayed significantly greater underachievement in math while 12 year old boys displayed more reading problems 3. 12 year old girls displayed overachievement 4. Majority displayed only minimal or moderate underachievement in reading & math but equal numbers fell into all 4 categories for spelling 5. 33% had deficits of 1 year or more with spelling deficits more common *6. Most subjects who were deficient showed generalized underachievement rather than a specific disability
K-ABC Woodcock-Johnson Psychoeducational Battery Woodcock Language Proficiency Battery	Separate discrepancy calculations for 6 of 7 possible areas of LD computed via true score difference method (Berk, 1984) Categorization into 1 of 3 groups based on criteria for severe	1. Overall low achievement characterized ED group with standard scores ranging from 60–99 2. Severe ability-achievement discrepancy was prominent in the ED students with 31% having a general achievement discrepancy,

(continued)

35

TABLE 2–2.
Academic Problems of Emotionally Disturbed Students *(continued)*

Source	Subjects	Characteristics	Focus
Gallico (1985)			

priately, teachers seeking certification in these areas must be trained in academic remediation as well as behavior management and therapeutic techniques.

Problems and Implications Regarding Behavior Management

Much attention has been recently focused on the social/emotional problems of learning-disabled students. Studies comparing this group's behavioral difficulties to those reported for disturbed students indicate that learning-disabled students are likely to need specific programming to deal with their behavior. Although the problems of emotionally disturbed students may be more frequent and severe, the same kinds of conduct difficulties, such as, noncompliance, aggression, and defiance, commonly effect the learning-disabled student's classroom performance.

Tests Used	Methods	Results/Conclusion*
	discrepancy: (1) underachievement (2) equivalent achievers (3) overachievers	41% had discrepancy in reading recognition, 54% in comprehension, 51% in overall reading, 24% in arithmetic, 39% in written language & 27% in oral language 3. Overachievement existed in 3% of the students with 17% in reading recognition, 2% in comprehension, 10% in overall reading, 10% in arithmetic, 15% in written expression, & 15% in oral language 4. 66% of ED students had overall achievement equivalent to cognitive ability *5. A significant number of ED students would meet a stringent criteria for a severe ability-achievement discrepancy characteristic of LD students

* These large-scale studies cannot easily be condensed; see original work for specific subject and method information.

In-depth assessment of the emotional and behavioral functioning of learning-disabled students should be conducted along with academic and cognitive evaluations. Diagnosticians must define more clearly what types of behavioral problems are likely to be secondary to the learning disability (for example, hyperactivity and distractibility) and what types of emotional problems are independent of, but coexisting with, the learning disability.

In conclusion, it appears that mental health professionals involved with emotionally disturbed children and special educators concerned with the learning disabled have much to offer each other in planning programs to meet these students' needs. The need for interdisciplinary cooperation has never been greater. To meet this challenge, medical, psychological, and educational personnel must be willing to go beyond the barriers of their own disciplines and share their knowledge and expertise.

TABLE 2–3.

Behavior Problems of Learning-Disabled Students

Source	Subjects	Characteristics	Focus
Nichol (1974)	232 children randomly selected from 1,037 children From the 232, 20% randomly chosen for follow-up	Age under 18 All children lived in metropolitan Vancouver, Canada	Survey of LD students referred to psychiatrists over a 5 year period
Epstein, Cullinan, & Rosemier (1983)	559 LD boys matched samples of non-LD boys	Age elementary school IQs normal Severe achievement deficits Normal sensory acuity Normals came from same schools as LD students	Patterns of behavior problems
McConaughty & Ritter (1985)	123 boys referred for learning problems	Ages 6–11 IQs 77+ to 85 (N = 10) 85+ (N = 113)	Social competence of LD boys
Gallico (1985)	40 LD students boys girls	Ages 6–12–6 Mean IQs 86 All students in	Behavior problems of LD students

Tests Used	Methods	Results/Conclusion*
School records reviewed	Follow-up on random samples with review of records	1. Referrals for academic problems represented 22% of all cases seen by psychiatrists 2. Boys outnumbered girls by 5 to 1 3. Second most frequent complaint was behavioral disturbance
Behavior Problem Checklist (Quay & Peterson)	Factor analysis	1. Considerable similarity across normal & LD groups on 3 of 4 2. Normal students essentially replicated previous studies 3. Results of LD students, while similar to normals, revealed substantial differences in social competence, anxiety, & attention deficits *4. Hyperactive behavior should be discriminated from aggressive & conduct problems in LD students
WISC-R Child Behavior Checklist (Achenbach) Parent Report Form	Analysis of variance Subgrouping by IQ pattern	1. IQ did not relate to overall severity of behavior problems 2. LD boys showed less social contact with friends, organization, less participation in activity, & lower school performance 3. Behavior problems rating was within the clinical range for severity *4. LD boys experienced more problems in social competence & behavior than expected
Child Behavior Checklist — Teacher Report	Multivariate analysis of variance	1. LD students mean for total behavior problems, externalizing & internalizing

(continued)

TABLE 2-3.

Behavior Problems of Learning-Disabled Students *(continued)*

Source	Subjects	Characteristics	Focus
Gallico (1985) *(continued)*		special education school for LD All students from an urban setting	
Epstein, Bursuck, & Cullinan (1985)	316 LD boys 225 LD girls 77 LD girls	Ages 12–18 Ages 6–11 Ages 12–18 All students with average IQ, severe achievement deficits Normal sensory acuity All placed in public school special classes or resource rooms	Behavior problem patterns of older LD boys & girls
Slate & Sandargas (1986)	14 LD 14 Average	3rd, 4th, 5th graders Average grade level achievement, adequate peer relations, no medical problems LD IQ 84–102, at least 1 standard deviation between ability & achievement Achievement 60–83 All mainstreamed No medical problems	Comparison of LD & average students in regular classrooms

Tests Used	Methods	Results/Conclusion*
Form (Achenbach)		problems well above the 85th percentile with 23% scoring in the clinical range (98th percentile) for externalizing problems *2. Behavior problems increase in severity as the degree of LD increases
Behavior Problem Checklist (Quay & Peterson)	Principal components factor analysis	1. Conduct, anxiety, & inadequacy factors emerged for older boys similar to other studies but with no separate attention deficit factor 2. Conduct & anxiety emerged for younger girls 3. Conduct problems appeared for all three groups & was responsible for the greatest amount of variance 4. Age & sex differences revealed a change in quality of attention problems with age as well as the emergence of delinquent problems in older children
State-Event Classroom Observation System (Sandargas & Creed)	Direct observation for 10 weeks Time sampling Frequency format Multiple regression Discriminant analysis	1. LD students did not exhibit marker behaviors that varied from average 2. LD involved in academic tasks as much as AV 3. LD & AV students interaction with teacher time did not vary 4. Teacher behaviors, however, were different *5. Teachers may treat LD students differently once the student is classified

*These large-scale studies cannot easily be condensed; see original work for specific subject and method information.

Peer and Family Relations of Learning-Disabled Children

*I*n writing about peer and family relations, Hartup (1981) noted that children are together and interacting all around us, but that "the contributions of peer interaction to the child's capacities to relate to others, to regulate emotional expression, and to understand complex social events is not well-understood" (p. 280). Hartup maintained that the familial world and the world of children interact to influence the growth of social competencies. Additions, extensions, and elaborations of parent-child modes of interaction appear to develop in the child's second social world, that is, in the peer culture. Moreover, Minuchin (1974) described what competencies are effected by children's experiences within the "sibling subsystem" of the family:

> Within this context, children support, isolate, scapegoat, and learn from each other.... Children learn how to negotiate, cooperate, and compete. They learn how to make friends and allies, how to save face while submitting, and how to achieve recognition of their skills. They may take different positions in

their jockeying with one another, and those positions, taken early in the family, can be significant in the subsequent course of their lives [both inside and outside of the family]. (p. 59)

It is within these contexts, then, that learning-disabled children will be considered in this chapter — the peer culture and the familial world. Some of the questions that will be explored include:

1. Are learning-disabled children "at risk" for later developmental problems?

2. What factors associated with learning disability might contribute to adaptation in childhood and adult society?

3. What is the social status of learning-disabled children and what is the nature of their social behaviors?

4. What is the nature of family functioning in families of learning-disabled children?

5. Are there etiological factors that contribute to varying social competencies of such children?

6. What is the stress on the family with a learning-disabled child?

LONG-TERM PROGNOSIS OF LEARNING-DISABLED CHILDREN

The educational and psychiatric prognoses of children with learning disabilities appear to be unfavorable in many regards. For example, Werner & Smith (1982) highlighted the results of a longitudinal study of a multiracial cohort of nearly 700 children, born on the island of Kauai, who were followed through the second decade of their lives:

Among children in need of placement in a learning disability class by age 10 years, serious problems persisted throughout adolescence. Agency records of four out of five indicated continued academic underachievement, confounded by absenteeism, truancy, a high incidence of repetitive, impulsive acting-out behavior that led to problems with the police for the boys and sexual misconduct for the girls, and other mental-health problems less often attended to. Rates of contact with community agencies were nine times as high as that for control-group youths matched by age, sex, socioeconomic status, and ethnicity. (p. 33)

Werner also reported that at age 18 most of these children displayed continued perceptual-motor problems, deficiencies in verbal skills, and serious underachievement in reading and writing. Additionally, self-reports uncovered a pervasive lack of self-assurance and interpersonal competency. Few children (25 percent) were rated as improved at this age. Given such compelling evidence, it appears that learning-disabled children are likely "at risk" for later developmental problems. However, it remains unclear at this time what specific factors associated with learning disability contribute to multiple adjustment problems throughout childhood and adolescence and continuing into adult life.

One possible explanatory variable, posited by Yule and Rutter (1985), is severe reading disability. For example, in the Isle of Wight studies (Rutter, Tizard, & Whitmore, 1970), one-quarter of the children with specific reading retardation showed antisocial behavior, and one-third of conduct-disordered children were reading-retarded. Yule and Rutter (1985) pointed out that the association is not just with delinquency, but with nondelinquent aggressive and antisocial behavior as well. The nature and meaning of these associations are addressed in their consideration of two hypotheses: (1) that educational failure leads to low self-esteem, emotional disturbance, and antagonism toward school, which may contribute to disturbances of conduct, and (2) that both reading difficulties and disturbance to some extent show a common etiology (e.g., detrimental social or familial variables or temperamental characteristics). Rejecting any single explanation for the association between reading retardation and psychiatric disorder, they noted that the relationship is stronger with antisocial disorders than with emotional disorders. They also concluded that temperamental characteristics (e.g., overactivity) may often predispose children to both disorders, that in some cases, school failure may lead to a lowering of self-esteem, which contributes to conduct problems, and that "adverse family influences may also play some role in the genesis of both disorders" (p. 453). The occurrence of problems in the families of learning-disabled children in particular will be discussed subsequently, but there is considerable evidence of family dysfunction among the families of "special educational children" in general. For example, high rates of marital disturbance, abuse in the family, and parent history of psychiatric disorder have been found for children referred for potential placement in classes for children with social and emotional disturbances (Mattison et al., 1986). Similar reports have indicated that special education teachers perceive moderate to severe degrees of psychological morbidity in the families of their students (Morse, Cutler, & Fink, 1964). Most important, however, is an emerging literature that suggests that parent-child interaction in the home may influence the child's behavior in school — his or her school achievement and social functioning (Hess

& Holloway, 1984; MacDonald & Parke, 1984). For example, in a non-clinic sample of young adolescents, their interactions with their fathers were significantly related to school behavior (as measured by a behavior problem checklist completed by teachers) and academic performance or grade point average (Forehand, Long, Brody, & Fauber, 1986). In questioning this cause-and-effect sequence, Forehand and colleagues hypothesized that when conflicts between fathers and adolescents occur, they may disturb the adolescents' school performance. Alternatively, when the adolescents get poor grades, fathers (perhaps more often than mothers) may take the children to task, resulting in increased conflict. Similarly, the depression levels of mothers were significantly related to school behavior problems, possibly due to the fewer resources that depressed mothers have for parenting. Single-parent settings notwithstanding, such data indicate that home variables significantly predict school behavior and performance.

PEER RELATIONSHIPS OF LEARNING-DISABLED CHILDREN

This case example is descriptive of a particular learning-disabled child's difficulty with peer relationships.

Case Study #2: Social Competence of a Learning-Disabled Boy
Dale was a 10 year old boy who was not well-liked by his peers in school. He was a boy with average intelligence, but he could not read at the level of his classmates, nor could he perform well at mathematics. Dale had been identified as learning disabled through educational testing after a referral had been made by a teacher from a previous year. He received special resource help in both reading and mathematics. Dale tended to ask for help in class more often than other children. When he did not get the teacher's attention immediately, he often "goofed-off" or made the other students laugh. Dale disliked school, felt "dumb," and was perceived that way by most of his peers. One way he fought against this stigma was to play well at sports, for which he achieved some notoriety. However, Dale's teachers noticed that he was socially immature — he seemed more comfortable with boys who were younger or with boys who were equally unpopular. With boys and girls alike, Dale had attempted to participate in the popular circles and had largely met with rejection or was ignored. His attempts to join groups of popular boys playing board

games, for example, seemed awkward. He seemed to try to "move-in" too quickly and he sounded negative and bossy. Sometimes, he withdrew and gave up. At other times it seemed as if the children would not allow him to enter their games, no matter what he did.

Anecdotal evidence such as this, and research evidence as well, suggest that learning-disabled childen in general have experiences very similar to the experience of Dale. The focus of this chapter is on the variables that might contribute to the social competence of learning-disabled children.

ARE LEARNING-DISABLED CHILDREN "AT RISK" FOR PROBLEMS IN ADJUSTMENT TO LATER LIFE?

If it is true that learning-disabled children lack the skills to initiate and promote positive relationships with other children, then they may be "at risk" for problems in adjusting to later life. Indeed, a large body of research with primates convincingly demonstrated the role that early peer contact plays in the development of a wide range of later competencies, including the modulation of aggression, and the expression of adaptive mating behaviors (Hartup, 1981; Suomi, 1979). In human social development, it has been speculated by Gottman and Parkhurst (1980) that, to some extent, peer-group attachments may compensate for poor parent-child relationships. When social interaction is deficient (as indexed by sociometric status, observational indices, or other objective ratings), the development of behavioral and emotional disorders becomes more likely. For example, Roff, Sells, and Gaden (1972) studied a sample of 40,000 children in 21 cities and found that, except for the lowest socioeconomic class, a highly positive relationship was observed between low peer acceptance score and delinquency four years later. Unpopular children have also been found to be more likely to receive bad-conduct discharges from the armed forces (Roff, 1961) and to drop out of school (Hartup, 1970; Ullman, 1957). Cowen, Pederson, Babigian, Izzo, and Trost (1973) demonstrated that unpopular children show a disproportionate tendency toward mental health problems, reflected by their overrepresentation in a community-wide psychiatric register. Moreover, children with low levels of peer acceptance are more likely to be poor academic achievers (Bonney, 1971). Clearly, then, research suggests that peer acceptance influences *all* children's normal growth and development. For this reason, social competence among learning-disabled children has been scrutinized very closely in recent years.

ARE LEARNING-DISABLED CHILDREN ALSO SOCIALLY DISABLED?

Gottlieb, Gottlieb, Berkell, and Levy (1986) observed that the bulk of the literature agrees that "learning disabled children are socially disabled as well" (p. 619). Similarly, in their investigation, learning-disabled boys and girls were observed to play alone on the playground more than their non-learning-disabled peers. However, their findings revealed as well "that the lower sociometric status of learning disabled children is the result of same-sex rejections by girls; no differences in cross-sex ratings between learning-disabled and non-learning disabled classmates on in same-sex ratings by boys were found to exist" (p. 621). Gottlieb and colleagues (1986) posited that the commonly identified inferior social status of learning-disabled children (about 8 to 10 years of age) may be correct only for girls. In a review, Dudley-Marling and Edmiaston (1985) argued against the low social status commonly ascribed to learning-disabled children and adolescents and rejected previous research (on statistical grounds), which had concluded that learning-disabled girls were at greatest risk for unpopularity. They found that studies using the peer-nomination technique, as well as studies using peer- or teacher-acceptance scales, generally supported the conclusion that learning-disabled students, as a group, enjoy relatively low social status among their peers. Note that the results of a recent study by Gresham and Reschly (1986) also indicated that teachers, parents, and peers rated mainstreamed learning-disabled children (aged 7 years 6 months to 11 years 6 months) as deficient in task-related, interpersonal, and self-related social skill domains. Learning-disabled children were also more poorly accepted by peers in play and work situations. Dudley-Marling and Edmiaston (1985) contended, however, that few learning-disabled students are rejected, some are popular, and most enjoy neutral status — that learning-disabled individuals are only at greater risk for social rejection than non-learning-disabled peers. Additionally, they asserted that observational studies suggest few differences in the frequency and quality of learning-disabled and non-learning-disabled childrens' and adolescents' interactions with their teachers or their peers. From a methodological point of view, Dudley-Marling and Edmiaston (1985) eschewed the future use of group design research for the ethnographic study of interactions of individual learning-disabled students within specific, naturalistic contexts. Their critique is compelling in its assertion that basic research is needed to assess the contribution of peers, teachers, parents, and academic failure to the social development of learning-disabled individuals before they, by themselves, can be assumed to "have the problem." Even if social competence problems reside, for the most part, with the learning-disabled child, there are exceptions. For example, there is evidence that adolescents with learning disabilities are as popular as nonhandicapped pupils among the students that actually know them (Sabornie & Kauffman, 1986). Similarly, Perlmutter, Crocker, Cordray, and Garstecki (1983) showed that although learning-disabled high-school students, as a group, scored significantly below nonhandicapped regular-class peers in peer rating scale sociometric status, there was a small subgroup of learning-disabled students who scored in the same range as the most popular nondisabled students.

SUMMARY OF THE CONTROVERSY ON SOCIAL DISABILITY IN LEARNING-DISABLED CHILDREN

Several important points can be gleaned from the outlined controversy. It is obvious that, as a group, learning-disabled students are not alike in every way. They are no more homogeneous than other specific groups of children. For example, not all gifted and talented children are universally well-liked. But learning-disabled children may share some common difficulties.

There is considerable evidence that they may often experience social failure, or at best, social anonymity. Admittedly, most of this evidence is culled from research with groups of children, rather than individuals. However, many teachers and clinicians report, anecdotally, the same kinds of social problems among their learning-disabled students and clients as described here. More sophisticated and creative research methods are needed in order to give a picture of learning-disabled children which is broad in scope. Moreover, researchers should focus not only on normative data, but also on children who are exceptions to the group norm. It would be very interesting, for example, to compare the social interactions of learning-disabled children who are exceptionally popular among their classmates with those of less-popular learning-disabled children. How do popular learning-disabled children overcome what seem to be inherent social difficulties (based on cognitive- or language-processing problems)? It would also be informative to know if learning-disabled children who are generally unpopular among their classmates have a single "best friend." If they do, then it perhaps suggests that different criteria are needed to assess their social skillfulness.

Many variables extraneous to the individual, learning-disabled child may contribute to low social status. For example, a child's reputation as a poor student, or his or her physical strength or attractiveness may add to, or diminish from, his or her popularity. Other variables have been identified in the child development literature that contribute to social status. For example, Gottman, Gonson, and Rasmussen (1975) posited a "group membership" hypothesis that states that once a child has been perceived as popular or unpopular it becomes very difficult for that child to be viewed differently by peers even when he or she behaves in a manner that should disconfirm his or her previous reputation. Conversely, Bryan (1974) found that learning-disabled students retained their unpopularity from one year to the next, even though classroom composition had changed.

For this reason, the interactions of learning-disabled children with their peers need to be studied such that the whole fabric of their peer relationships can be viewed. The implications for the treatment of social skills deficits in learning-disabled children are many if it is discovered that their "peer systems" ignore or even discourage competent behaviors and reinforce incompetent ones (see Chapter 6 for a discussion of contextual issues in therapy). An even larger issue is the role of families in enabling learning-disabled children to assume socially competent behaviors. This issue will be addressed in the section to follow. The additional question of whether there is such a phenomenon as "familial" language-learning disabilities, in which dysfunctional communication is modeled by parents and adopted by children should be considered.

Despite all the qualifiers mentioned previously, there appears to be "abundant evidence indicating the social dysfunction of learning disabled children" (Ginsburg, 1985, p. 25; Gresham & Reschly, 1986). The following is a partial list of dysfunctional social behaviors attributed to learning-disabled children and reported in the literature:

- Learning-disabled children were more negativistic, competitive, and rejecting in their interactions, and were less considerate than non–learning–disabled children (Bryan, Wheeler, Felcan, & Henck, 1976).
- Learning-disabled children were deficient in social skills such as greeting others, conversing, listening to others, smiling and laughing, and complimenting others (LaGreca & Mesibov, 1981).
- Learning-disabled children did not change their mean length of utterance to suit a variety of situations (Soenksen, Flagg & Schmits, 1981).
- Learning-disabled children emitted more personal, egocentric statements than a comparison group (Soenksen et al., 1978)
- Learning-disabled children did not make eye contact as much as a control group (Bryan, Sherman, & Fisher, 1979)
- Learning-disabled children were less accurate in their perception of nonverbal communication (e.g., Bryan, 1977)

Moreover, in a study in which learning-disabled and nondisabled children viewed videotaped interactions, made inferences about an actor's emotions, and identified affective inconsistencies, Ginsburg (1985) characterized learning-disabled children and the origins of their nonsocial behaviors in the following manner:

> They are children who have difficulty in sustaining attention and in inhibiting their impulses. They tend to misperceive environmental stimuli and misunderstand the social behaviors of their peers. Poorly developed social-cognitive skills result in withdrawn and isolated behavior as well as aggressive acting out. These behavior problems serve to isolate them further and expand the downward spiral. (p. 67)

It is clear then, that the social repertoire of learning-disabled children is problematic in many respects. It is unclear, however, if such deficiencies can be ameliorated with singular treatments of the learning-disabled child out of context (for example, in individual, behavioral, cognitive-behavioral, or insight-oriented therapies). Whatever are the spiraling, dysfunctional interactions of learning-disabled children and their peers, each participant in the interaction is likely to play a part that needs to be recognized and challenged in situ. When this idea is understood by teachers, clinicians, and researchers, then steps can be taken in the classroom, therapy office, and elsewhere so that the learning-disabled child can experience himself or herself as socially competent, and his or her peers as allies in that process.

FAMILY FUNCTINING OF FAMILIES WITH LEARNING-DISABLED CHILDREN

It has been observed by Furstenberg (1985) that within the discipline of child development, the child has often been portrayed as "a discrete entity, analytically distinct from the external social environment" (p. 281). Ignoring the relationship between family systems and child development, the field had viewed children as biological and psychological entities, dislocated from the "collective needs and interests" of the family. Similarly, study of the learning-disabled child has, for the most part, relied heavily on mechanistic and individualistic conceptual models. More complex models have recognized that the development of the learning-disabled child is regulated by the family system and vice versa. Minuchin (1974) explained the contextual model in the following way:

> The individual influences his context and is influenced by it in constantly recurring sequences of interaction. The individual who lives within

a family is a member of a social system to which he must adapt. His actions are governed by the characteristics of the system and these characteristics include the effects of his own actions. The individual responds to stresses in other parts of the system to which he adapts; and he may contribute significantly to stressing other members of the system. The individual can be approached as a subsystem, or part, of the system, but the whole must be taken into account. (p. 9)

Wilchesky and Reynolds (1986), in an excellent discussion of this issue as it relates to social competence, identified three major etiological factors in the development of social interactional problems of learning-disabled children: (1) "(constitutional) factors directly associated with the learning disability," e.g., basic psychological processing and/or expressive deficits; (2) the secondary effect of school failure — that is, experiencing academic failure puts the child at high risk for developing poor self concept; and (3) "family interaction patterns (which) also play a role in maintaining the maladaptive behavior" (p. 412), though all learning-disabled children are not assumed to live within dysfunctional families. Rather, it is consistent with all systems orientations to assume that "a boy having trouble in school is not having trouble alone" (Aponte, 1976). What does the research on the families of learning-disabled children uncover with regard to child and family interactions?

In their review, Fish and Jain (1985) found a paucity of such research. Notably, most of the research focused on the pathological nature of the interactions between the learning-disabled child and his or her family and ignored what might be "healthy" or ameliorative interactions between them. Mothers were variously described as enmeshed, overengaged, and overly dependent on their learning-disabled child, but as accepting the child's disability. Note that the psychological and psychiatric literatures are replete with blame for mothers for any number of child disorders. It is consistent with such "mother-blaming" literatures that mothers are described currently as pathologically involved with their learning-disabled children, rather than as "very close," a less-caricatured and value-laden descriptor. Fathers were described as underinvolved, self-derogatory, unsatisfied, and denying of the child's problem, as well as disengaged and neglectful. Together, the parents of learning-disabled children were viewed as having unresolved conflicts about academic achievement, and as taking a much longer time in making a decision (in conjunction with their learning-disabled child) in comparison to normal families, indicating a lack of conflict resolution and problem-solving skills. Additionally, each parent was described as undermining the efforts of the others. It was further suggested that marital conflict often develops in learning-disabled families, which only exacerbates the problems already associated with the learning disability. Fish and Jain (1985) summarized a common perspective in the literature — "that the child is an extension of the parent's images, hopes and aspirations, and the identification of the child as 'learning disabled' causes a grief or loss reaction in the parents. Each parent goes through the phases of denial, anger, and self-blame (and) reacts in his or her own way to deal with feelings of helplessness encountered in such a situation. They may either reject or overprotect the child as a way of suppressing their own anger or guilt. As the anxiety of the parents mount, so does the anxiety of the learning disabled child which then may be manifested in the very symptom of learning disability" (p. 592–593). Better-adjusted families of learning-disabled children were described by Jain and Zimmerman (1984) as cohesive, as having a strong parental coalition, and as having mothers and fathers who were equally as likely to be participants with their learning-disabled child. Also, the child's disability was clearly and openly accepted in these families, but not allowed to overshadow the child's other competencies. The child was assisted in finding methods for compensating for his or her specific disablilties. Nonetheless, parental limits and expectations for the child's academic and social spheres were made explicit.

SUMMARY

Whereas previous literature identified only the learning-disabled child as problematic, recent literature has hypothesized that the learning-disabled child is inextricably involved in a web of interconnecting, and perhaps symptom-maintaining, relationships with both his or her peer group and family. The hypothesis states further that as the family (or peer group within a classroom, for example) transacts across time, the members communicate verbally or nonverbally, constantly creating feedback loops or patterns (Plas, 1986). From this perspective, the family or peer group is held together by these communication patterns or rules which control the system. Within the classroom peer group, one such rule might be "Do not respond to Steven's requests or demands (or those of any similar child with low status among his classmates) in a way that would indicate that you take him seriously." Children in Steven's peer group might operationalize this rule by laughing at Steven, ignoring him, or by never establishing eye contact with him. Conversely, Steven might indirectly promote this injunction by expressing himself in a way that ensures that he is not taken seriously. His conversation might be tangential to what is being talked about at the moment, or the things he talks about might sound pretentious (he depicts himself as a computer expert, for example). Or he may continually undermine the seriousness of what he says by smiling when he speaks. Similarly, within the family, one shared assumption or rule might be "James has the same problems in math as his father had when he was in school, and therefore, we do not expect James to do well in math or to routinely complete his homework." Again, a complicated set of behaviors may support such an injunction within the family. A dance is performed by the problem child with other family members who follow one another's leads through subtle — and sometimes not-so-subtle cues — such that faulting a particular family member or members or directing efforts for change at a particular person in the family may ignore the cooperation inherent in the dance. At times, fault must be found with individuals — as in the case of sexual abuse of children or spousal abuse. More often, an awareness of the process among family or peer group members, in addition to recognition of the individual learning-disabled child's capacities, must inform efforts at therapeutic change in order for them to be effective. The implications of such hypotheses for the treatment of the learning-disabled child will be discussed in Chapter 6.

The Medical and Psychiatric Perspective

Psychiatric Disorders of Children and Adolescents: Diagnosis

*C*urrently, there is a trend for school personnel involved with special needs students to have increased contact with child psychiatrists and other mental health professionals (Forness & Cantwell, 1982). The growing use of mental health assessments makes it necessary for educators to develop a knowledge of diagnostic terminology and treatment recommendations. As it was explained in Chapters 1 and 2, a strong relationship between learning disabilities and pyschiatric, or emotional, disturbances has also been demonstrated. It has become evident in many research studies that not only do learning disabilities predispose to emotional problems, but many psychiatric disorders themselves impair attention and impede the learning process (Hunt & Cohen, 1984).

DSM-III

Whereas educators use P.L. 94–142 as their standard, the *Diagnostic and Statistical Manual,* third edition, (DSM-III) (American Psychiatric Association, 1980) is the medical standard reference for the classification of psychiatric disorders of childhood. This system of classification is used by child psychiatrists and other mental health professionals for assessment and reports. A knowledge of the basic organization of the DSM-III is necessary for educators to fully understand the psychiatric evaluations obtained on students. (A revised manual, the DSM-III-R, is scheduled for publication in mid–1987. A listing of relevant childhood diagnostic criteria is provided in Appendix C).

The DSM-III provides the necessary criteria for making reliable diagnostic judgments. Reliability and validity studies of DSM-III diagnoses have been established to a far greater degree than any previous classification system (Cantwell, 1985). The DSM-III system of classification is divided into five axes. Each axis will be globally reviewed and a case study will be presented to illustrate how the DSM-III is utilized.

Axes I Through V

On *Axis I,* all clinical psychiatric syndromes are coded, other than specific developmental and personality disorders, which are listed on Axis II. The DSM-III system provides such details as duration of illness, frequency and intensity of symptoms, associated features, age of onset, course and outcome of the disorder, predisposing factors, complications, degree of impairment, prevalence, sex ratio, familial pattern, and differential diagnosis.

Axis II is composed of personality disorders, which are usually not diagnosed until late adolescence, and the specific developmental disorders. The specific developmental disorders of Axis II include areas of learning disabilities such as reading, arithmetic, and language. The DSM-III defines the specific developmental reading and arithmetic disorders as performance on standardized, individually administered tests of reading skill or arithmetic achievement which are significantly below the expected level. "Expected level" is determined by the individual's schooling, chronological age, and mental age.

Axis III codes any physical disorder or conditions relevant to the understanding or management of the child's psychiatric problem. For example, a child may have both bronchial asthma and a separation anxiety disorder, and may manipulate teachers or parents with his or her condition, or experience a true asthmatic attack when in a highly stressful situation. This factor would complicate management.

Axes IV and V allow the opportunity for special clinical or research settings to use more specific descriptions. Axis IV codes the overall severity of psychosocial stressors related to the psychiatric disorder. Examples include change to a new school, birth of a sibling, divorce of parents, and death of a close relative. These stressors play an important role in the prognosis or outcome and are therefore given special consideration. The DSM-III provides a rating scale for psychosocial stressors with clinical examples relevant to a child's or adolescent's life. Axis V assesses the individual's highest level of adaptive functioning within the past year. The scale ranges from "superior" to "grossly impaired." It identifies an optimal baseline to which the child's functioning will return if his or her psychiatric condition resolves. The following case is an example of how the DSM-III multiaxial system might be applied.

Case Study #3: Psychiatric Problem in a Boy with Reading Disorder

Billy, a 12 year old boy, was referred to a mental health consultant because of increasing oppositional behavior in the classroom, angry and explosive outbursts, and a decline in academic motivation. Investigation revealed that Billy had had reading difficulties since early elementary school. Also, he was hospitalized at the beginning of the current school year and was diagnosed as having juvenile-onset diabetes mellitus. Subsequent to this hospitalization and the establishment of the diagnosis of diabetes, Billy began to withdraw from his old friends and ended his involvement with activities that he had previously enjoyed. Interviews with his parents revealed that Billy would not cooperate with his insulin treatments, and that he frequently expressed a "wish to die."

The DSM-III multiaxial diagnosis for this case would very likely appear on the psychiatric report as follows:

Axis I:	Major depression, single episode
Axis II:	Developmental reading disorder
Axis III:	Diabetes mellitus
Axis IV:	Psychosocial stressor (hospitalization and diagnosis of chronic medical illness) Severity 5 — Severe
Axis V:	Highest level of adaptive functioning in past year: 3 — Good

LEARNING AND PSYCHIATRIC DISORDERS

In recent years, there has been some clinical evidence of a strong relationship between learning disorders and serious emotional disturbances (Hunt & Cohen, 1984). An assessment of children referred for psychiatric evaluation to the UCLA Neuropsychiatric Institute yielded a 75 percent association with serious deficits in academic achievement (Cantwell & Forness, 1982). This study demonstrates that children who exhibit emotional disturbances need to be evaluated for learning difficulties as well.

The Importance of Language Development

Appropriate language development is essential for the healthy growth of learning skills and social-emotional competence. Children with significant language disorders will be at high risk for both learning and psychiatric disorders. A study designed to investigate the association between developmental language disorders, learning disabilities, and psychiatric disorders identified the classroom rather than the home as a particular location for overt behavioral disturbances (Cantwell & Baker, 1980). Other studies have noted that children with developmental reading disorders are likely to have significant psychiatric disorders (Rutter, 1974). For a child with a specific developmental disorder, early educational frustration and failure often sets the stage for emotional and behavioral disturbances. Future research may confirm the suspicion that early assessment and treatment of developmental language disorders could prevent not only the development of learning problems, but lessen the likelihood of psychiatric disorders as well.

A recent study at the University of North Carolina in Chapel Hill linked the presence of specific language disorders in children with known emotional disturbances. A thorough language assessment was performed on 40 child psychiatry impatients (Gualtieri, Koviath, & Van Bourgondien, 1983). Over half of the patients in the study, with different psychiatric diagnoses, were assessed as having moderate to severe developmental language disorders. More than one quarter of the sample had significant language deficits. The researchers concluded that language disorders may be as common in child psychiatry populations as psychiatric symptoms are among groups of children with developmental language disorders.

LEARNING DISABILITIES AND PSYCHOSOCIAL DEVELOPMENT

In addition to the academic limitations and emotional disturbances associated with learning disabilities, there are also influences on psychosocial development. During adolescence, the presence of a learning disability often has a negative effect upon the individual's self-concept (Cohen, 1985). The adolescent tends to view himself or herself as "inadequate and damaged," experiencing feelings of helplessness and humiliation. As the school setting becomes an area of pressure and distress, the child will avoid it in order to protect his or her self-esteem. Therefore, psychosocial factors are considered an important adjunct of early educational identification and interventions of learning disabilities. Those working with the learning disabled need to be aware that the self-esteem of these students is quite vulnerable, and may be quickly overwhelmed by feelings of inadequacy and failure. Children with learning disabilities will often require substantial psychosocial intervention to enhance their coping skills and increase their likelihood of success. Such interventions will be discussed in Chapter 6.

LEARNING DISABILITIES AND DEPRESSION

Another area to consider is the relationship between academic underachievement and depression. As previously stated, the presence of learning difficulties erodes self-esteem. This may increase the child's vulnerability to depression. On the other hand, a true depressive disorder may be mistaken for a learning disability, as some of the signs are similar. The depressed child has diminished mental energy, impaired concentration, poor motivation to achieve, and an overall deterioration in school performance. Teachers may mistakenly assess a poorly functioning child as having a "learning problem," failing to note that the decline in academic performance was secondary to a depressive disorder (Colbert, Newman, Ney, & Young, 1982). Once such a child is accurately diagnosed as being depressed and is provided with appropriate psychiatric treatment, academic performance should also improve.

NEUROPSYCHIATRIC AND COMMUNICATION DISORDERS: PERVASIVE DEVELOPMENTAL DISORDER, AUTISM, AND CHILDHOOD SCHIZOPHRENIA

The definition and the assessment of profoundly incapacitating conditions seen by child psychiatrists have been very controversial in the past. Considerable clarification occurred with widespread implementation of the DSM-III diagnostic criteria. However, difficulties still exist in distinguishing between the autistic and pervasive developmental disorders and schizophrenia in childhood.

Pervasive Developmental Disorder

Pervasive developmental disorder is a descriptive label for individuals who have sustained profound abnormalities in development. Severe impairment is seen in areas of socialization, language, intellectual functioning, and emotional capacity. Such conditions are so disabling that special education facilities are required in almost all cases.

In 1943, Leo Kanner, of the Johns Hopkins Hospital, first defined the syndrome of infantile autism. By DSM-III criteria, infantile autism is described as the most severely disabling pervasive developmental disorder. However, prior to DSM-III diagnostic standardization, confusion existed when some degree of psychosis was assessed in the child. Until recently, most psychotic disorders in children were diagnosed as childhood schizophrenia. The term *psychotic* indicates gross impairment in reality testing. The affected individual is unable to accurately evaluate his or her perceptions and thoughts, making inaccurate assumptions about external reality (Rapoport & Ismond, 1984). Such overlapping of diagnostic boundaries was corrected by DSM-III criteria, allowing childhood schizophrenia and the pervasive developmental disorders (including infantile autism) to be firmly established as separate diagnostic entities.

Infantile Autism

Kanner, in his landmark paper (Kanner, 1943), noted certain distinguishing features in children he labeled *autistic*. He described such unique characteristics as their lack of ability to develop relationships with other people, extreme aloofness, insistence on preserving "sameness," simple and repetitive patterns of play, lack of imaginative capacity, and disturbances in language (including slow acquisition and strange use of speech). Kanner noted that this autistic syndrome originated during infancy; thus, the term *infantile autism*. Strong evidence has accumulated that the autistic syndrome first described by Kanner is different in origin and expression from the psychotic disorders commonly seen in adults (Tsai, 1986).

The syndrome of infantile autism is the most severe of the pervasive developmental disorders. The age of onset is prior to 2 years 6 months and can often be traced to the first few months of life. It is marked by a massive distortion of skills and functions that are normally acquired during this time. Profound disabilities exist in the areas of language function and social and environmental responsiveness. The most marked characteristic is the lack of responsiveness to other human beings. These infants fail to cuddle, avoid eye contact, do not smile responsively, do not enjoy affection, fail to develop cooperative play, fail to develop friendships, mechanically cling to specific adults, and interact with adults indiscriminately. Older children are generally unable to engage in imaginative play or participate in cooperative play. Infantile autism is also marked by gross impairment in communication and language development. Up to 50 percent fail to develop any speech (Ricks & Wing, 1976). When speech does develop, it often is extremely abnormal. Peculiar patterns develop, such as echolalia (the meaningless repetition of sounds or words) and pronominal reversal (in particular, referring to another as "I" and to oneself as "he"). Words and phrases are used idiosyncratically, and mechanical production of speech is often oddly impaired (Tsai, 1986). Nonverbal communication, including meaningful gaze and gesture, is also deficient and is generally not utilized to convey information. Autistic children also demonstrate bizarre responses to the environment. These may include resistance to change, interest in or attachment to peculiar inanimate objects, or severe ritualistic or compulsive behavior (i.e., repetitive touching). To fulfill the diagnostic criteria for infantile autism, the child must be without the presence of delusions, hallucinations, loosening of associations, and incoherence, all of which are present in schizophrenia.

Childhood-Onset Pervasive Developmental Disorder

Childhood-onset pervasive developmental disorder refers to an extreme and incapacitating disturbance in human relations and to a wide range of bizarre behaviors, developing as a full syndrome *after* the age of 2 years 6 months, and prior to the age of 12 years. As with infantile autism, a formal thought disorder, delusions, and hallucinations are absent. The current DSM-III diagnostic criteria for childhood-onset pervasive developmental disorder emphasize that there is a gross impairment in social relationships. These children do not develop normal attachment behaviors and fail to achieve interpersonal bonding. Impairment may include inappropriate clinging, a lack of appropriate emotional responsiveness, and a lack of empathy. Three of the following seven features must be present to fulfill the DSM-III diagnostic criteria:

1. *Excessive and unexplained anxiety.* These children often exhibit such symptoms as free floating anxiety, catastrophic reactions to everyday occurrences, an inability to be consoled when upset, and unexplained panic attacks.

2. *Diminished, constricted, and inappropriate affect.* In addition, one may observe in such cases a noticeable lack of appropriate fear reactions, as well as unexplained rage and extreme mood changes.

3. *Sustained resistance to change.* Catastrophic reactions may follow even minor changes in everyday routine (i.e., altering an automobile route, or changing dinner time).

4. *Oddities of motor movement.* Upon inspection, these children often demonstrate peculiar posturing, peculiar hand or finger movements, and walking on tip-toe.

5. *Speech abnormalities.* Children with a pervasive developmental disorder are frequently noted to speak with a question-like melody or monotonous voice.

6. *Abnormal sensory and perceptual experiences.* In reaction to either soft or loud noises, these children respond with hyposensitivity or hypersensitivity to hearing (i.e., hypo- or hyperacusis).

7. *Self-injurious behaviors.* Of serious concern is the fact that children with this disorder are particularly prone to overt self-mutilation (i.e., self-biting or -hitting, severe head banging).

Long-term studies indicate that children with the pervasive developmental disorders, particularly infantile autism, have a very poor long-term outcome. These individuals may remain severely incapacitated as they become older, with only a minority able to become free from totally dependent lifestyles. Even those with some social independence and a lesser degree of impairment will still continue to need substantial supervision in the social, educational, and vocational spheres (Goldfarb, 1980). Prognosis is poorest for children who, by the age of 5 years, are still mute and unable to communicate with language. It is generally agreed that the most important prognostic indicator is the child's IQ (Eisenberg, 1958; Goldfarb, 1980). Approximately 70 percent of patients with diagnosable infantile autism will be classified as mentally retarded by the time they reach adulthood (Rutter, 1970).

The origin of pervasive developmental disorders is still unclear, although it appears that many of these children have organic brain syndromes. Many neurological disorders are reported to be associated. They include cerebral palsy, lead encephelopathy, tuberous sclerosis, and a variety of different seizure disorders. Investigators identified a strong association with prenatal, perinatal, and neonatal complications. A variety of infections, both in utero and shortly after birth, have been implicated. Some of the more common infectious agents identified include congenital rubella, toxoplasmosis and cytomegalovirus (Tsai, 1986). The role of genetic inheritance in the development of autism has also received attention. Some known genetic disorders, including phenylketonuria (PKU) and the fragile X syndrome, are sometimes linked with autism. Studies have also indicated an approximately one-third concordance of autism with identical twins and a zero concordance with fraternal twins. Folstein and Rutter (1977) examined the importance of a biological hazard leading to possible brain injury and concluded that autism may occur as a result of brain injury or through a combination of brain injury and genetic vulnerability.

One area in need of clarification is the purported psychogenic etiology of autism. In his original description of autism, Kanner (1943) speculated that a causative role in the pathology was the particular personality styles of the child's parent(s). The mothers in particular were described as emotionally cold and aloof. Thus, the term *ice box* or *refrigerator mother* was conceived, to the great disservice of these overwhelmed parents. Subsequent, well-controlled studies have been unable to substantiate this causative theory (Ornitz & Ritvo, 1976). It is very likely that the emotional "coldness" Kanner observed was not the cause of, but rather the response to, the frustrating, unrewarding, and exhausting experience of parenting an autistic child.

Childhood Schizophrenia

As mentioned earlier, the degree to which schizophrenia is present in childhood has been an area of great controversy in recent years. It was once believed that all psychotic illnesses during childhood were an early expression of schizophrenia. However, it is now known that childhood schizophrenia represents only a small number of such cases of childhood psychoses. There is substantial evidence that autism and childhood schizophrenia are entirely separate disorders (Rutter, 1978). In fact, *childhood schizophrenia* has been deleted from the DSM-III. Instead, the formal DSM-III adult schizophrenia diagnostic criteria must be fulfilled in order for a child to be classified as schizophrenic (Campbell, 1984; Kydd & Werry, 1982). Therefore, childhood schizophrenia is described as being nearly identical to adult schizophrenia, with the same characteristics present. They include delusions, hallucinations, loosening of associations, and incoherence. Such features are not found in autistic children. Furthermore, the onset of childhood schizophrenia is later than that of autism. Onset of this disorder prior to early puberty (age 11) occurs only rarely (Goldfarb, 1980).

The DSM-III criteria for a schizophrenic disorder emphasize that there is a severe degree of deterioration from a previous level of functioning in such areas as work, school, self-care, and social relations. The illness must be present continuously for at least 6 months. A similar illness of a shorter duration is considered to be either a brief psychotic reaction (if less than 2 weeks), or a schizophreniform disorder (if between 2 weeks and 6 months). The formal diagnostic criteria require that at least one of the following six items be present during a phase of the illness:

    1. *Bizarre delusions.* These thought disturbances have no possible basis in fact, such as, delusions of being controlled, thought broadcasting, thought insertion, and thought withdrawal.

    2. *Nonparanoid delusions.* These may include somatic, grandiose, or other delusions without persecutory or jealous content.

    3. *Paranoid delusions.* These delusions with persecutory or jealous content are accompanied by hallucinations.

    4. *Auditory hallucinations.* In some cases, the schizophrenic child reports that he or she hears one voice that keeps talking about his or her thoughts or behavior, or several voices that converse with each other.

    5. *Auditory hallucinations.* In other cases, the disturbed child reports hearing voices with content of more than one or two words, and that have no apparent relation to depression or elation.

    6. *Incoherence, marked loosening of associations, markedly illogical thinking, or marked poverty in content of speech.* These severe thought disturbances are considered to be symptomatic of schizophrenia if they are associated with either blunted, flat, or inappropriate affect, delusions or hallucinations, or catatonic or other grossly disorganized behavior.

Case Study #4: Pervasive Developmental Disorder

    Patricia, a 6 year old girl, was brought to the child mental health consultant by her parents following a conference with the kindergarten teacher. The teacher informed them that Patricia behaved in a peculiar manner, ignoring and appearing to be oblivious to other children. She had frequent intense anxiety and panic episodes, in which she would be very agitated, cry, or bolt out of the classroom. These episodes could neither be explained by environmental circumstances nor could the intervention of the teacher calm her down.

    The parents stated that Patricia, their only child, always seemed "different" from other children, and had trouble "fitting in with the neighborhood kids." As a result, they had not enrolled her in preschool. They also reported that, in their opinion, Patricia had developed "normally" until the age of years, when they become aware of certain peculiarities, including a monotonous voice quality, unusual echoing of what others had said, and a tendency to become preoccupied with waving her fingers in front of her face. *Diagnosis:* Childhood-onset Pervasive Developmental Disorder.

INTERNALIZING DISORDERS: DEPRESSION AND ANXIETY DISORDERS

The internalizing disorders of childhood are disturbances in emotions and feelings. The most frequent internalizing disorders in children are depression and separation anxiety. The vulnerability of a child experiencing one or both of those disorders is determined by his or her biogenetic endowment, as well as by a stressful home environment. The accurate assessment of an internalizing disorder of childhood enables an appropriate mental health referral and initiation of effective treatment.

Childhood Depression

The existence of childhood depression as a true disorder has been a controversial issue. It was once believed that children, because of their cognitive and emotional immaturity, did not possess the capacity to be depressed (Rie, 1966). However, numerous studies have demonstrated that depression can indeed exist in children and even in infants.

Harmon (1982) corroborated the important findings of the early work of Rene Spitz (1946) on institutionalized infants and young children. Spitz developed his concept of anaclitic depression by observing infants separated from their biological mothers and placed in an institution. Many of these infants, deprived of maternal bonding, developed withdrawal, apathy, excessive weeping, weight loss, sleep disturbance, delayed developmental milestones, and impaired physical growth. Most devastatingly, they appeared to have higher illness and mortality rates. This finding and its later validation have firmly established that a child deprived of early nurturing and attachment may experience a profoundly disruptive and devastating depressive state.

The presence of depression in older children and adolescents has also gained increasing recognition. In the past, adolescence was viewed as a time of inevitable turmoil and the signs of depression were often overlooked. Whereas an adult may simply state that he or she feels sad or hopeless, a child is more likely to act out his or her dysphoric (unhappy) mood. The concept of "masked depression" was emphasized in the late 1960s by Kurt Glaser, a Baltimore child psychiatrist and pediatrician (1968). He noted that many children with such "acting out" behaviors as aggression, school avoidance, precocious sexual activity, and drug and alcohol use were actually depressed. Rather than showing the classic symptoms of depression, they used the only means they had available, their overt behavior. By treating the actual depression, the behavior tended to improve.

Recent research has investigated the relationship between conduct disorders and underlying depression. A study at Columbia University found that more than one-third of children and adolescents with diagnosed depression also had a conduct disorder (Puig-Antich, 1982). Many of these patients, when treated with antidepressants, improved both emotionally and behaviorally.

The use of DSM-III criteria has advanced the detection of major depression in children and adolescents. When such diagnostic criteria are properly applied, a fairly accurate assessment of the presenting disorder can be made (Cantwell, 1980; Cantwell, 1983; Carlson, 1986). As the DSM-III criteria are the standardized guide for establishing a diagnosis of depression, they can be useful to educators in assessing possible underlying mood disorders in their students.

The presence of a depressed or dysphoric mood is most important to establishing the diagnosis of major depression. Though unable to express it, depressed children appear upon careful visual observation to be distinctly unhappy (Poznanski, 1982). They tend to have an expressionless, fixed look of sadness, with only fleeting smiles or other brief changes in facial expression. By DSM-III criteria, major depression is associated with anhedonia, or the loss of interest or pleasure in usual activities. Anhedonia in a child is particularly noticeable, as "having fun" is a crucial element of a child's life, and a necessary component of play and learning. Chronic boredom, when associated with anhedonia in a child, may suggest depression. Dysphoria is further characterized by feeling sad, blue, hopeless, low, "down in the dumps," and irritable. By DSM-III standards, the mood disturbance must be present for at least 2 weeks, and must include four of the following eight symptoms:

1. *A significant change in appetite.* The depressed child may have a poor appetite, often with associated weight loss or failure to make expected weight gain. Or there may be substantial increase in eating, often compulsively, with an associated gain in weight.

2. *Sleep disturbance.* Insomnia is characterized by difficulty in falling asleep or, of greater concern, early morning awakening with

inability to fall back to sleep. Hypersomnia, or excessive sleep, is often seen in the younger populations.

3. *Psychomotor agitation or psychomotor retardation.* A child with moderate or severe depression generally demonstrates diminished motor activity. He or she may sit or stand with a slouched posture, staring vacantly ahead. Children with milder forms of depression may display increased motor activity. There is also a relative retardation, or slowing of speech, in a significantly depressed child.

4. *Anhedonia.* The depressed child usually suffers from the incapacity to experience enjoyment in activities that were once pleasurable. The anhedonic child is often bored, morose, and withdrawn from the surrounding world.

5. *Loss of energy and complaints of excessive fatigue.* The depressed child will not have the energy level necessary to take part in the normal activities appropriate for his or her age group.

6. *Feelings of worthlessness, low self-esteem, and excessive or inappropriate feelings of guilt.* The depressed child has an extraordinarily poor self-image, regardless of how others may view him or her.

7. *Diminished ability to think or concentrate.* In children, this is often expressed as an impairment in school performance. Deterioration in performance of a child who had previously done well in school may be the first sign of a depressed state. In addition to difficulty concentrating, the child has a lack of interest in school work and a noticeable lack of motivation to achieve well and receive praise.

8. *Recurrent thoughts of death, suicidal ideation, or actual suicide attempt.* The depressed child is often preoccupied with morbid thoughts, imagining himself or herself as the victim. This may lead to acts of self-harm, including overt suicidal behavior.

In recent years, there has been increased sophistication in diagnosing depression in children. Earlier and more accurate assessments can now be made. There is new evidence that the true frequency of depressive illness, particularly in adolescence, is increasing (Earls, 1984). As a result, greater efforts have been made to understand the full extent and impact of depression in the young. One critical finding recently established the increased risk for depression in the offspring of depressed parents (Weissman, Prusoff, & Gammon, 1984). Such evidence reinforces the need for early intervention in childhood depression and for assessment and treatment of the depressed parent(s). A comprehensive approach is essential so as to minimize the risks for severe disability and impairment in vulnerable children.

Childhood Suicide

In the past 20 years, the rate of adolescent suicide has increased by 200 percent, and over the past 30 years by 300 percent. Considering that "accidental" death is often rooted in self-destructive intent, the true suicide rate for adolescents may be even higher. In addition, there is a surprisingly high occurrence of suicidal thinking and behavior in younger children. Traditionally, there has been great reluctance to acknowledge suicide in children. However, recent clinical investigations provide strong evidence to the contrary. In spite of their cognitive and emotional immaturity, young children are fully capable of deliberately taking their own lives. Recent reports describe that some children as young as 2 years 6 months or 3 years demonstrate dangerous suicidal tendencies (Rosenthal & Rosenthal, 1984). Other studies of elementary school–age children have assessed greater suicidal risks than expected for this age group. In-depth interviews of child psychiatry inpatients showed a surprisingly high prevalence of 75 percent for past suicidal behavior (Pfeffer, Solomon, & Plutchik, 1982). Among a sample of children who were psychiatric outpatients, 33 percent had a history of suicidal behavior (Pfeffer, Conte, Plutchik, & Jerrett, 1980). And perhaps the most astounding finding, 12 percent of children without a history of psychiatric disturbance, treatment, or symptoms were detected to harbor suicidal thoughts or had displayed suicidal acts (Pfeffer, Zuckerman, Plutchik, & Mizruchi, 1984). Factors cited in these studies that distinguished suicidal from nonsuicidal children were the child's depression, hopelessness, worthlessness, wishes to die, intense preoccupation with death, viewing death as temporary and pleasant, and parental depression and suicidal behavior. Perhaps the strongest risk factor was a history of parental suicide. Other investigators indicated previous suicidal behavior, drug and alcohol abuse, antisocial behavior, and parental violence and abuse as commonly present in the histories of children who took their own lives (Shafti, Carrigan, Whittinghill, & Derrick, 1985).

Relationship of Depression to Suicide

Depression is identified as the most frequently associated psychiatric disorder among suicidal victims of all ages. Studies demonstrate that for individuals with a major depressive illness there is a 30 times greater likelihood of completed suicides than in the general population (Guze & Robbins, 1970). Investigators have also shown the strong association between depression and suicidal behavior in children (Pfeffer, 1986). Consequently, early identification and treatment of depression in children may potentially alleviate much of this serious risk.

Suicidal behavior in a child may be perceived by parents and other adults as so threatening and frightening that it is often denied or ignored, causing the underlying pathology to worsen. Retrospective studies of children who had committed suicide reveal previous suicidal behavior. When an initial suicidal gesture fails to elicit proper intervention, the child is at risk of becoming increasingly hopeless, and is more likely to proceed to more serious and lethal behavior. As parents and teachers become sensitized to the warning signs of childhood depression, and particularly self-destructive behavior, there is a better chance that treatment will be accessible, and the likelihood of tragic outcome reduced.

Separation Anxiety Disorder

Separation anxiety is an emotional disorder of childhood that is common in the early elementary school years. It has been identified as the primary factor in 80 percent of all cases of school phobia (Gittelman & Klein, 1984). However, separation anxiety is a normal developmental process during the first few years of life. It becomes pathological *only* when it intrudes upon normal functioning, learning, and growth.

Separation anxiety disorder equally affects boys and girls and is evenly distributed among all socioeconomic classes (Jaffe & Magnuson, 1985). Pathological separation may occur in children with a prior history of chronic difficulty separating from major attachment figures (i.e., parents or other primary caregivers). It can also develop in a child with previously healthy functioning who had shown no prior signs of unusual separation anxiety. Separation anxiety disorder, unlike many other emotional disorders in children, does not necessarily follow a chronic and intractable course. It may end spontaneously without leaving any residual impairment in the child (Gittelman, 1984).

The role separation anxiety plays in school phobia has been known for many years (Eisenberg, 1958). There is a difference, however, between a child who is unable to attend school because of an incapacitating anxiety condition and the child whose school truancy is related to antisocial behavior. In making such a distinction, it is apparent that the school truant is not avoiding school so as to stay at home and be in close contact with an important attachment figure (i.e., his or her mother). Instead, the truant child willfully avoids school for reasons quite independent of any painful or disturbing internal state.

For children with true separation anxiety, school refusal becomes a primary expression. The morning hours, when it is time to prepare for school, become a period of heightened anxiety and fear. Such children often complain of a variety of disabling physical symptoms. It is not unusual for these children to become combative and physical over going to school. (Folstein, 1986). Academic performance, intelligence, and past development are usually normal in these children. However, social adjustment is frequently poor (Hersov, 1960).

Before reviewing the diagnostic criteria for separation anxiety disorder, it is important to briefly discuss what is meant by the term *anxiety*. Anxiety is defined as a pervasive feeling of apprehension, discomfort, dread, or fear that something catastrophic will occur in the near future. This feeling of anxiety occurs in the presence of an unrealistically heightened fear of future events. In addition, there is an exaggerated and distorted response to a relatively mild and unremarkable external stressor. In response to the perception of impending danger, the individual believes himself or herself to be helpless and unable to master or control the situation. Physical symptoms often include labored and difficult breathing, a sense of respiratory constriction, a rapid heart rate, and an accelerated breathing rate that may precipitate hyperventilation. Other problems include difficulties with sleep, irritability, complaints of lack of energy, nausea and vomiting, abdominal pain, and headaches (Werkman, 1980).

The DSM-III criteria for separation anxiety disorder specify that the associated signs and symptoms have a duration of at least 2 weeks. For separation anxiety to exist, the DSM-III diagnostic criteria require at least three of the following nine symptom clusters:

1. *Fear of parental injury and/or abandonment.* The child maintains an excessive and unrealistic state of fear that some danger or harm will affect one of his or her major attachment figures. The child will also often harbor the fear of abandonment by his or her caregiver.

2. *Fear of harm to self.* The child will have an intense and unrealistic fear that some unanticipated yet unpreventable catastrophic event will occur (i.e., being lost, kidnapped, killed, or involved in an accident), which would then create the inevitable separation from his or her major attachement figure.

3. *School refusal.* The child will refuse to let his or her major attachment figure out of sight, and will refuse to go to school so as to maintain close physical proximity.

4. *Sleeping with parent.* The child will be unable or unwilling to sleep alone, and consequently will demand to sleep with his or her

major attachment figure. Similarly, the child will be unable to sleep away from home, or away from his or her major attachment figure.

5. *Physically clinging to parent.* The child will insist upon following his or her major attachment figure around the home, and will express vehement opposition and intolerance at being left behind, even for a brief period of time.

6. *Nightmares.* The child will report frequent nightmares centered around the theme of separation.

7. *Frequent somatic complaints.* The child will complain bitterly of a variety of physical symptoms (i.e., nausea and vomiting, abdominal pain, and headaches), in relation to anticipated attendance at school or upon entry into a school setting. Monday morning is a particular time when complaints of severe and incapacitating somatic symptoms will be voiced.

8. *Panic when anticipating parent separation.* When imminent separation from a major attachment figure is anticipated, the child will engage in displays of marked and excessive distress, including violent temper outbursts, profuse crying, or pleading to prevent the impending separation.

9. *Profound sadness when forced to separate from parent.* When not in the presence of his or her major attachment figure, the child will display significant degrees of sadness, apathy, and social withdrawal, as well as difficulty in concentrating on work or play activities.

The degree to which a child may experience an episode of separation anxiety disorder is variable. Disorders may be mild, where the child experiences only a passing or occasional concern about separation, and is able to function in a setting away from his or her major attachment figure. Or, the disorder may be moderate, with the child experiencing panic reactions to separation but is still able to function adequately for a period of time. And finally, the disorder may be severe, with the child experiencing paralyzing panic reactions to threatened or actual separation. Such panic events are incapacitating and force the child to strongly protest any separation from his or her major attachment figure.

Case Study #5: An Example of Separation Anxiety

Louis, a 10 year old boy, was taken to a mental health consultant after refusing to attend school for the first two and a half months of the fifth grade. Louis's mother informed the consultant that her son constantly follows her around their home, becomes panic stricken at the thought of his mother leaving the house without him, pleads tear-

fully to be allowed to accompany her "to make sure" she
will be safe, and complains of incapacitating aches and pains
when the suggestion is made that he return to school. Upon
questioning, Louis's mother revealed that her husband had
deserted her six months ago for another woman and that
over the past several weeks, Louis had insisted that she
allow him to sleep with her during the night.
Diagnosis: Separation Anxiety Disorder

EXTERNALIZING DISORDERS: CONDUCT DISORDER
AND ATTENTION DEFICIT DISORDER WITH HYPERACTIVITY

The externalizing disorders of childhood are disturbances in behavior. The most common experienced by children are the conduct
disorders and attention deficit disorder with hyperactivity. These disorders may exist concurrently in the same child or may occur in isolation from one another. The externalizing disorders are particularly
apparent to those who work with children of elementary school age.

Conduct Disorders

Conduct disorders are the most common cause for referral of
children for psychiatric evaluation and treatment and pose a serious
problem for teachers and society. Aggressive conduct disorders are one
of the major pediatric public health problems in the United States
(O'Donnell, 1985).

In spite of the widespread prevalence of conduct disorders, causative factors are varied, and effective treatment remains elusive. Consequently, the prognosis for such cases is generally poor. A considerable
proportion of children with childhood conduct disorders develop alcohol abuse and antisocial personality disorders as adults (Stewart, 1986).

The behavior of children with conduct disorders is either
aggressive, antisocial, or a combination of both. The most severe and
identifiable disorders among school children are of this latter category.
DSM-III criteria divides conduct disorders into four subtypes, based
upon the presence of absence of aggressive and antisocial (or undersocialized) behaviors.

Aggressive Conduct Disorders

These are defined by DSM-III as repeated violations of the basic
rights of others. Examples are acts of physical violence against persons
or property, or robbery by the use of threat or violent force.

Aggressive conduct disorders have been the focus of interest of investigators studying school-related problems. Studies demonstrate that the onset is generally by the first year of elementary school, with aggressive symptoms relatively stable and persistent throughout childhood and adolescence (Stewart & deBlois, 1985). Aggressive conduct disorders are relatively common throughout the population and occur four times as frequently in boys as girls (Stewart, de Blois, Meardon, & Cummings, 1980). Both boys and girls with aggressive conduct disorders appear to have difficult and oppositional temperaments. Traits apparent at an early age include poor impulse control, low tolerance for frustration, impatience, and easy excitability (Stewart, 1986).

Both social and biological factors play a role in the development of conduct disorders. Early parenting technique is identified as a major factor predicting later aggressive and delinquent behavior (Loeber, 1983). Early patterns of aggression also predict later delinquent behavior. Aggression and delinquent behaviors are generally associated with parental rejection, broken homes, poverty, and overcrowding. Many fathers of children with conduct disorders are physically abusive towards their wives and children (O'Donnell, 1985).

Nonaggressive Conduct Disorders

These behavior disturbances involve the persistent pattern of violating important rules at home or at school (i.e., frequent truancy, substance abuse, repeated short-term running away from home, persistent lying, and acts of nonviolent theft.

Socializing versus Undersocialized Conduct Disorders

DSM-III further distinguishes between the socialized and undersocialized conduct disorders. Nonsocialized disorders are marked by the lack of sustained peer-group friendships, the refusal or inability to extend oneself for others without immediate gain, lack of guilt or remorse, blaming or informing on companions, and lack of concern for the welfare of others. By DSM-III definition, such behavior patterns must be present for at least 6 months.

Strong evidence points to a genetic role in conduct disorders (Jary & Stewart, 1985). Studies indicate that most boys with conduct disorders have fathers who had conduct disorders as children. These men have persistent antisocial disorders and a strong likelihood of abusing alcohol. Although this may appear to be an environmental influence that is learned, such behavioral patterns in the child may exist even when the father leaves home before the child is born.

Conduct Disorders and Brain Dysfunction.

Children with conduct disorders, particularly those with aggressive characteristics, often have a history of serious medical and neurological illness. They are far more accident-prone than their peers, and are often victims of significant perinatal problems (birth injury), head and face injuries, and physical abuse (Lewis, 1985). Recent studies show that a surprisingly high percentage of boys with histories of aggressive behaviors also have major neurological abnormalities, including seizure disorders (especially psychomotor epilepsy). These neurological vulnerabilities appear to have made the individuals more prone to violence, impulsiveness, poor school performance, and overall maladaptive behavior (Lewis, Shanok, Pincus, & Glaser, 1979).

The role underlying organic brain disturbance may play in triggering episodic aggressive acts is only marginally understood. Nevertheless, the efficacy of anticonvulsant medications in reducing aggressive behavior in selected populations has been established (O'Donnell, 1985). Anticonvulsant medications, particularly carbamazepine (Tegretol) and diphenylhydantion (Dilantin or Phenytoin) have proven to be effective not only in conduct-disordered children with known seizure disorders, but also in those in whom underlying brain dysfunction is only suspected. Seizure disturbances involving the temporal lobes of the brain (known by several names, including temporal lobe epilepsy, psychomotor epilepsy, or complex-partial seizure disorder) seem to predispose a child to periodic episodes of aggressive and irritable behavior. In children and adolescents with a known history of seizure disorder, head trauma, or perinatal crisis, careful neurological examination and consideration of treatment with anticonvulsant medications is recommended.

Cognitive deficits are also associated with conduct disorders. Studies link childhood aggressive and antisocial behavior to low IQ, specific reading disability, articulation disturbances, and delayed language development (Stewart, 1986). In addition to psychosocial and psychiatric treatment, it is often necessary to provide these children with special education intervention.

Conduct Disorder and Depression

Recent attention has been given to the association between conduct disorder and depression. Over the past several years, there has been more evidence of an association between juvenile delinquency and depression (Alessi, 1984). Another study that looked for major depression in children unexpectedly detected a prevalence of conduct disorders in one-third of the subjects. Treatment of the depression also improved the conduct disorder symptoms (Puig-Antich, 1982). Such revealing data demonstrate the need to assess children with conduct disorders for the presence of underlying depression. Evidence is increasing that depression may predispose an individual to develop a conduct disorder. If future studies corroborate a close link between conduct disorders and depression, considerable progress may be made in testing this difficult condition with the use of antidepressant medication.

Outcome studies have generally revealed a poor prognosis for children with conduct disorders. Some studies show that up to 50 percent of these children develop some degree of antisocial disorder in adulthood (Graham & Rutter, 1973). Early childhood aggression has also been identifed as a predictor of adolescent alcohol abuse and delinquency (Kellam, Ensminger, & Simon, 1980). Severity of disturbance and early onset are factors that make it more likely that serious aggressive and antisocial problems will persist in adulthood.

Treatment of conduct disorders may be approached from a variety of perspectives. Ideally, a combination of different therapeutic models may optimize response. Behaviorally structured treatment, involving both the home environment and the classroom, is often essential. Special training is necessary to motivate parents of these children to learn how to reshape their child's behavior through the use of external reinforcers and controls. Teachers will need specialized training in how to structure the classroom and create a system of rewards and contingencies in response to targeted behaviors. Children also need individualized training in social skills and impulse control (see Chapter 6 for a comprehensive discussion of treatment).

A comprehensive approach to treating children with conduct disorders includes providing the parents with necessary support. In addition to coping with the stressors of caring for and managing such disruptive children, parents are often in need of specialized mental health treatment. As the mothers, in particular, may be prone to chronic low-grade depression, appropriate psychiatric intervention is often necessary.

Attention Deficit Disorder and Hyperactivity (ADDH)

A common disorder in children easily observable in the classroom setting is the clustering of behaviors known as the *attention deficit disorders,* both with and without hyperactivity. Attention deficit disorder with hyperactivity (ADDH) is far more common. Attention deficit disorder is characterized by developmentally inappropriate short attention span and impulsive behaviors. Excessive motor activity may or may not be present, a feature that serves to distinguish between these two children subtypes. ADDH is commonly considered to spontaneously fade away and remit by late adolescence. However, recent follow-up surveys on individuals diagnosed with these disorders have revealed that in a significant percentage of cases clinically identifiable syndromes will persist into adulthood. In particular, the inattentive and impulsive components of the syndrome persist into adulthood, and clinically appear as what is defined as the attention deficit disorder, residual subtype. Signs of motor overactivity, however, generally do not persist into adulthood and consequently are not associated with this subtype (Greenhill, 1985).

The incidence of attention deficit disorders and hyperactivity is assessed at being between 5 to 10 percent of all school children in the county (Cantwell, 1975; O'Quinn, 1985). In special education classes, the proportion of children with diagnosible attention deficit disorders and hyperactivity will often approach the 50th percentile. This condition is predominately present in the male population, with a boy to girl ratio in the range of 10 to 1. When examining family histories, it is common to observe a clustering of such conditions in the male members of the family (Cantwell, 1972).

A careful history taken from the child's parents, particularly the mother, often reveals that many signs of the disorder first presented by the age of 3 years. In fact, mothers often recall that their child had engaged in more activity in utero (as compared to siblings), was more irritable as an infant, and displayed more climbing and running behaviors as a toddler (Greenhill, 1985). However, parents usually do not feel the behavior is abnormal until the child enters the classroom setting, when easy comparisons are made to other children.

In the past, attention deficit disorders and hyperactivity conditions carried many labels, based upon the belief that they were caused by some degree of organic brain damage. In the early 1970s, many disruptive behaviors observable in the classroom were grouped together under the heading *minimal brain dysfunction* (MBD). Advocates of this theory maintained that attention deficit disorders and hyperactive behavioral patterns were part of a diffuse, mild neurological disorder. Upon reexamination, this is now viewed by some as inappropriate and overly simplistic, and criticized as having poor construct validity, low interrater reliablity, and poor predictive outcome (Shaffer & Greenhill, 1979). The so-called neurological soft signs (including abnormal reflexes, inability to carry out rapid alternating movements, and generally poor coordination), were once thought to be indications of minimal brain damage. However, they are now considered to be of little use in making the diagnosis (Shaffer, 1978).

The essential features of ADDH are relative to the child's mental and chronological age. They include the developmentally immature signs of inattention, impulsivity, and hyperactivity. These signs are objectively observable and are almost always reported by the significant adults in the child's environment. When a situation arises where the reports of parents and teachers conflict, primary considerations should be given to teacher reports, because of their greater familiarity with age-appropriate norms. The disorder is more easily observed in a group setting such as the classroom. Signs of this disorder may not be present when the child is subject to one on one supervision.

The DSM-III has identified the precise criteria for making a diagnosis of ADDH. Inattention is defined by the presence of at least three of the following five items:

1. *Failure to complete tasks.* Projects are often left unfinished, as the child abandons them in order to begin other activities.

2. *Difficulty listening.* The teacher or parent must repeat the verbal message several times before it is perceived and understood.

3. *Easily distracted.* The child often finds it difficult to maintain focus on an isolated task, especially when faced with a variety of competing sensory stimuli.

4. *Limited attention span.* The child frequently has great difficulty with schoolwork or other tasks requiring sustained attention. This makes it exhausting for both parents and teachers to assist the child in the learning process.

5. *Difficulty sustaining interest.* The child often has great difficulty maintaining interest in a play activity. Parents often report that their child will move excessively from one uncompleted play activity to the next. For example, the child may show a poor capacity to sustain his or her attention to even the most appealing television program.

Impulsivity is identified by the presence of at least three of the following six items:

1. *Acting before thinking.* The child acts without forethought of the consequences, appears to be "oblivious to danger," and takes dares.

2. *Difficulty sustaining involvement in the same activity.* The child moves rapidly from one activity to another.

3. *Disorganization.* The child has difficulty organizing his or her work (however, this is not due to any gross cognitive impairment).

4. *Need for structure.* The child requires a lot of supervision. From both home and school reports, it is frequently noted that the child cannot be left alone.

5. *Excessive speaking out of turn.* The child repeatedly calls out in class.

6. *Difficulty following rules.* The child has difficulty waiting for his or her turn in games or group situations, and often tries to substitute his or her own rules. Such uncontrolled behaviors often make these children unpopular and unaccepted by their peers. The rule-breaking behavior of these children is done in a thoughtless, unpremeditated manner. This is distinguished from the behavior of children who engage in more willfully provocative and planned violations of rules and regulations.

Hyperactivity is identified by the presence of at least two of the following five items:

1. *Excessive motoric activity.* The child has frequent episodes of excessively running about or climbing.

2. *Fidgetiness.* The child has difficulty sitting still or fidgets excessively.

3. *Inability to remain seated in controlled environment.* The child has difficulty staying seated.

4. *Excessive night-time movement.* The child moves about excessively during sleep.

5. *Constant movement.* The child is always "on the go" or acts as if "driven by a motor."

The DSM-III diagnostic criteria for attention deficit disorder with or without hyperactivity stipulates that the onset must have occurred prior to the age of 7 years, and that the duration at time of diagnosis must have been for at least 6 months.

There is a series of related features that are not included in the DSM-III criteria, but are often associated with ADDH:

1. *Personality features.* Children with ADDH are often observed to have particular personality characteristics. These include a low tolerance for frustration; frequent irritability; displays of obstinacy, stubbornness, and negativism; labile emotional reactions, including temper outbursts; poor tolerance to efforts at discipline; low self-esteem.

2. *Poor peer relationships.* Children with ADDH are frequently not well-accepted by their peers. They display chronic difficulty with group rules and structures, and consequently are often barred from games. Finding it very hard to abide by rules, they try to change them, usually in opposition to the group preference. Consequently, the child will become even more unwanted and unpopular. Both the peers and the teachers of these children usually have little success in setting effective limits for them.

3. *Aggressive Outbursts.* Children with ADDH often have explosive reactions to the excessive teasing they receive. Such fighting is usually impulsive and in reaction to the situation at hand rather than premediated.

4. *Poor Academic Performance.* Children with ADDH often perform quite poorly on classroom tests even if they are of normal or above-average intelligence. Their chronic inattentiveness is associated with a poor capacity to concentrate. Such children are prone to making careless mistakes and have poor organizational skills. Their maladaptive behavior styles in the classroom include such disruptive behaviors as inappropriate touching and bumping up against other students, calling out of turn, and excessive noise-making. These behaviors further detract from their poor capacity to stay on task. Furthermore, these children tend to score low on standardized testing, and may also have specific learning disabilities (especially those concerning reading and arithmetic skills). Such specific learning disabilities may further compound the children's academic underachievement, and heighten many of the negative features of the disorder. However, such specific learning disabilities will not be found in every child with ADDH who underachieves. Academic failure may very often be predominantly caused by inattention and misapplication of skills.

Case Study #6: An Example of an Aggressive Conduct Problem

Joey, an 8 year old boy, was the cause of great concern and exasperation for his third-grade teacher. During a visit to the school by a mental health consultant, Joey's teacher described him as a difficult behavior problem in the classroom. Joey had a limited capacity to remain seated during classroom activities, and frequently jumped out of his chair to run around the room and provoke other students. Joey was also described as being very disorganized with his school work, frequently calling out at inappropriate times, and alienating himself from his peers by his inability to comply with established game rules during recess. Finally, Joey's teacher described that he seemed to have a short attention span, was rarely able to complete an assignment, and was easily distracted from concentrating on a task when confronted with competing sensory stimuli.

After reviewing Joey's school work over the previous three school years, the mental health consultant noted that

Joey had been suspended from school several times for "beating up" smaller children, and on one occasion had been "caught" in the act of stealing a teacher's wallet. School records also indicated that Joey was very isolated from and unpopular with his peer group. He appeared to have established no close friendships.

Diagnosis: Attention Deficit Disorder with Hyperactivity. Conduct Disorder, Undersocialized, Aggressive

SUMMARY

A thorough understanding of childhood psychiatric disorders will be of great value to the educator. Collaboration between school personnel and mental health professionals is rapidly becoming more accessible. Developing effective and clear lines of communication is a critical step in optimizing the implementation of these necessary adjunct services.

Children with serious emotional disorders often create severe disruptions to the school environment. Understanding why such children behave in this manner demystifies this disturbing and often anxiety-provoking behavior. The ability to develop and refine the capacity to identify a child who presents with a significiant psychiatric disorder allow for the referral and treatment intervention appropriate for that child. Unfortunately, the majority of children and adolescents with genuine psychiatric disorders are rarely identified as such. Educators have a key position as the primary professionals interacting with children outside the home environment. In this capacity, they can play a vital role in mobilizing an evaluation and treatment process essential for the future health and well-being of these children.

Psychiatric Disorders of Children and Adolescents: Management Through Medication

S ince the 1950s, the field of psychopharmacology, the use of medications, has had a major role in the treatment of psychiatric disorders. Although specific medication treatment for the psychiatric disorders of childhood and adolescence has lagged somewhat behind the advances made with adult populations, substantial progress has been made over the past decade. During this recent period, knowledge from clinical and research studies has dramatically increased. Such gains in our understanding of drug mechanisms and how they effect specific psychiatric disorders allows for more effective treatments. The growing knowledge of potentially dangerous side effects of drug treatment enables safer medication planning to be devised. As our knowledge of such psychotropic medications increases, a healthy respect has developed for both the benefits and the potential dangers of these drugs.

It is important to note that psychopharmacology should never be the sole form of therapeutic intervention. Especially with children and adolescents, it is always an adjunct to some form of psychosocial treatment and educational intervention. A child or adolescent whose psychiatric disorder has been accurately diagnosed can be judiciously treated with an appropriate psychotropic medication. Such drug treatment may increase the effectiveness of the psychosocial therapy and hasten the resolution of the disturbance. Furthermore, coordination with the school program can only increase the likeihood of a successful outcome.

COORDINATING MEDICATION MANAGEMENT WITH EDUCATIONAL INTERVENTIONS

Experienced child psychiatrists and pediatricians have long realized that the schools may be valuable sources of information. Both with initial evaluations as well as monitoring ongoing treatment, consultation with the school often enables an optimal case outcome. Traditionally, the most frequent situation for school collaboration has been when a child with diagnosed attention deficit disorder with hyperactivity (ADDH) is receiving a stimulant medication (e.g., Ritalin). The functioning of a child with ADDH in the classroom setting is a key indicator of whether or not treatment has been effective. In addition to speaking directly with the child's teacher, the physician prescribing medication can obtain relevant and detailed teacher-based information through the utilization of one of a variety of child behavior checklists (see Appendix D). The most frequently utilized tool for data collection has been the Connors Rating Scale (Connors, 1969). The Connors Rating Scale is effective in eliciting information concerning degrees of impulsivity and inattention in the classroom. A more detailed data collection tool, although less commonly used, that provides more emphasis on the child's social behaviors in the Kendall Rating Scale (Kendall & Wilcox, 1979). Such teacher observation data, provided on a weekly basis, can be of great service to the physician in determining the relative effectiveness of treatment.

Although teacher observations of behaviors associated with ADDH are the most frequently requested by physicians, valuable information relevant to other internalizing and externalizing disorders of childhood can also be obtained. With the consent of the child's parent(s), the treating physician can learn much by opening up lines of communication with the schools. Teachers spend substantial periods of time with the child, have the advantage of contrasting a child's function across a broad range of childhood norms, and may be able to observe what specific alterations in function (both positive and negative) result from medication treatment. This school-based information is often of critical value to the physician in determining whether a child may benefit from medication treatment and whether or not the child undergoing treatment is receiving the optimal dosage or even the appropriate medication. Although the child and parent(s) remain the primary sources of information, the teacher is in a unique position to provide additional (and often previously unelicited) information concerning the functioning and treatment response of the child.

A series of charts have been prepared in order to provide an overview of what medications may be of particular value to the specific internalizing and externalizing disorders of childhood discussed in Chapter 4. Five charts are presented which review medication treatment of pervasive developmental disorder, major depressive disorder, separation-anxiety disorder, conduct disorder, and attention deficit disorder with hyperactivity. Children with one (or more) of these disorders may receive treatment with a variety of potent psychotropic medications. The charts that follow are designed for rapid and concise reference. For each disorder, a list has been arranged of general drug category, specific drug class, and both the generic (pharmacological) and trade names of each individual drug. The specific circumstances under which each medication may be indicated are described. The common side effects and potentially severe adverse consequences that may be precipitated during the course of medication treatment are also detailed.

PERVASIVE DEVELOPMENTAL DISORDER

The neuroleptic (or antipsychotic) medications are among the most potent drugs used in the treatment of psychiatric disorders. For children, their primary application is to reduce uncontrolled aggressive and self-injurious behaviors in pervasive developmental disorder, and to treat the delusions and hallucinations associated with the rare disorders of childhood schizophrenia. This category of medication has serious potential complications, and should only be applied with great caution (Table 5-1).

DEPRESSION

An accurate diagnosis of major depressive disorder usually necessitates treatment with an antidepressant medication. For patients who are carefully screened and monitored, the antidepressants are both safe and efficacious. Lithium treatment is indicated with more

[text continued on page 90]

TABLE 5-1.
Medications for Treatment of Pervasive Developmental Disorders (PDD)

Drug Category	Class	Generic Name (Trade Name)	Oral Dosage Range (mg)
Neuroleptics (Antipsychotics)	Butyrophenones	Haloperidol (Haldol)	1–12
	Thioxanthenes	Thiothixene (Navane)	2–16
	Phenothiazines	Chlorpromazine	10–250
		Thioridazine (Mellaril)	10–250
		Trifluoperazine (Stelazine)	1–16

Indications	Common Side Effects	Severe Adverse Consequences
Maladaptive behaviors (i.e., aggression, self-injury in PDD).	EPS (extrapyramidal symptoms), including brief but severe muscle spasms (acute dystonic reaction), variable degree of restlessness (akathisia) & drooling, tremor, muscle stiffness, reduction in spontaneous movement, lack of normal facial expression (pseudoparkinsonism).	Tardive dyskinesia (severe long-term movement disorders), including such signs as facial grimacing, fixed neck muscle spasm, writhing arm and shoulder movement, & respiratory grunting.
Delusions, hallucinations, & thought disorders in childhood schizophrenia.	Autonomic nervous system symptoms, including sedation, dry mouth, urinary retention, blurring of vision, & postural hypotension (a significant drop in blood pressure when standing up suddenly). Weight Gain.	Neuroleptic withdrawal syndrome, including emergent dyskinesias, restlessness, insomnia, headaches, abdominal discomfort, nausea, & vomiting.

TABLE 5–2.
Medications for Treatment of Depression

Drug Category	Class	Generic Name (Trade Name)	Oral Dosage Range (mg)
Antidepressants	Tricyclic (TCA)	Imipramine (Tofranil)	50–300
		Amitriptyline (Elavil)	50–300
		Desipramine (Norpramin)	50–300
		Nortriptyline (Aventyl)	25–150
	Monoamine Oxidase Inhibitor (MAOI)	Phenelzine (Nardil)	30–90
		Tranylcypromine (Parnate)	20–50
Mood Stabilizers	Lithium Salt	Lithium Carbonate (Eskalith or Lithobid)	150–2100

Indications	Common Side Effects	Severe Adverse Consequences
Signs & symptoms of depression, including persistently low mood, low energy, appetite & sleep disturbances, loss of interest or pleasure in usual activities (anhedonia), poor concentration, low self-esteem, excessive & inappropriate guilt & morbid self-destructive thoughts, & frequent tearfulness.	Autonomic nervous system symptoms, including dry mouth, postural hypotension, blurred vision, urinary retention, & sedation. Weight gain.	Cardiac arrhythmias.
	Postural hypotension, constipation, urinary hesitancy, muscle cramps, & weight gain.	Severe hypertension (high blood pressure) crisis if patient ingest certain foods (aged cheese, smoked fish, sausage, beer, red wine), or medications (stimulants).
Depressive signs & symptoms (see above) Manic or hypomanic signs & symptoms, including decreased need for sleep, more energy than usual, inflated self-esteem, disinhibition, physical restlessness, increased talkativeness, over-	Nausea, vomiting, diarrhea, abdominal discomfort, fatigue, & tremor.	Thyroid & renal (kidney) abnormalities.

(continued)

TABLE 5-2.
Medications for Treatment of Depression *(continued)*

Drug Category	Class	Generic Name (Trade Name)	Oral Dosage Range (mg)
Mood Stabilizers *(continued)*			

complicated cases that usually will not respond to antidepressants alone (Table 5-2).

SEPARATION ANXIETY

Although this condition may be approached from a variety of psychosocial perspectives, the medications discussed here often improve treatment response and hasten the resolution of the disorder (Table 5-3).

CONDUCT DISORDER

Conduct disorder is a more recently developed diagnosis, and consequently remains somewhat controversial. Recent studies have provided effective and (if properly utilized) safe adjunctive medication treatments. Note that the neuroleptics, because of their greater inherent risks, are not included as an appropriate medication for treatment of conduct disorder (Table 5-4).

ATTENTION DEFICIT DISORDER WITH HYPERACTIVITY

Although stimulants have been the traditional treatment approach for attention deficit disorders with hyperactivity, not all children will respond to these drugs. Consequently, a variety of alternative medication approaches have been developed (Table 5-5).

Indications	Common Side Effects	Severe Adverse Consequences
optimism, & excessive involvement in activities that have a high potential for painful consequences which are not recognized (i.e., sexual indiscretions, foolish buying sprees).		

SUMMARY

As diagnostic methods for childhood psychiatric disorders have become more accurate, adjunctive treatment with medication has developed greater refinement and specificity of action. Although all of the internalizing and externalizing disorders of childhood need to be addressed with psychosocial therapies, the judicious and timely application of medication often provides a superior overall treatment response. Treatment with psychotropic medications are not without risk, however, and should never be applied without accurate assessement of the underlying disorder and vigilant monitoring of drug effects.

TABLE 5–3.

Medications for Treatment of Separation Anxiety

Drug Category	Class	Generic Name (Trade Name)	Oral Dosage Range (mg)
Antidepressants	Tricyclic (TCA)	Imipramine (Tofranil)	50–200
Anxiolytics	Benzodiazepine	Alprazolam (Xanax)	¼–3

Indications	Common Side Effects	Severe Adverse Consequences
Excessive anxiety concerning separation from major attachment figure (usually a parent), often associated with school refusal.	(See chart on treatment of childhood depressive disorders.)	(See chart on treatment of childhood depressive disorders.)
(Same as above)	Sedation, paradoxial agitation, or excitement.	Withdrawal reactions, which may include the recurrence of severe anxiety. Seizures have been reported following the abrupt discrimination of higher dosages.

TABLE 5–4.
Medications for Treatment of Conduct Disorders

Drug Category	Class	Generic Name (Trade Name)	Oral Dosage Range (mg)
Mood Stabilizers	Lithium Salt	Lithium Carbonate (Eskolith, Lithobid)	300–2100
Antidepressants	Tricyclic (TCA)	Imipramine (Tofranil)	50–300
Anticonvulsants	Thymoleptic	Carbamazepine (Tegretol)	200–1600
		Phenytoin (Dilantin)	100–300
Antihypertensives	Beta-Adrenergic Blocker	Propanolol (Inderal)	30–300

Indications	Common Side Effects	Severe Adverse Consequences
Severe aggressive behaviors, including frequent impulsive violent acts, irritability, hositility, & explosive anger.	(See chart on treatment of childhood depressive disorders.)	(See chart on treatment of childhood depressive disorders.)
In some cases, depressive illness appears to predispose to the development of aggressive & deliquent behaviors.	(See chart on treatment of childhood depressive disorders.)	(See chart on treatment of childhood depressive disorders.)
Seizure disorders, especially temporal lobe epilepsy, may predispose to aggressive & irritable behaviors.	Drowiness, dizziness, abdominal discomfort, blood count abnormalities.	
	Nystagmus, a disturbance in eye movements, dizziness, gum hypertrophy (enlargement), & tremor.	
Although Propanolol is commonly used for patients with severe cardiovascular disease, it recently has been shown to be effective with episodic rageful & violent outbursts, especially if they appear to have been secondary to some prior episode of head injury.	Dizziness, fatigue.	Propanolol should not be given to patients with a history of diabetes, asthma, or congestive heart failure.

TABLE 5–5.

Medications for Use in Treatment of Attention Deficit Disorder with Hyperactivity

Drug Category	Class	Generic Name (Trade Name)	Oral Dosage Range (mg)
Psychostimulants	Amphetamine	Methylphenidate (Ritalin)	10–80
		Dextroamphetamine (Dexedrine)	5–40
		Magnesium Pemoline (Cylert)	18.75–150
Antidepressants	Tricyclic (TCA)	Imipramine (Tofanil)	25–200
		Amitriptyline (Elavil)	25–200
		Desipramine (Norpramin)	25–200
		Nortriptyline (Aventyl)	10–100
Antihypertensives	Alpha-adrenergic Agonist	Clonidine (Catapres)	0.05–0.3

Indications	Common Side Effects	Severe Adverse Consequences
ADDH, as manifested by signs of inattention, impulsivity, & hyperactivity.	Nausea, abdominal discomfort, anorexia, & insomnia.	A potentially serious side effect is the development of Tourette's syndrome. Any patient who develops facial or vocal tics must have their stimulant medicated discontinued.
(Same as above)	(See chart on treatment of childhood depressive disorders.)	(See chart on treatment of childhood depressive disorders.)
(Same as above)	Sedation, lethargy, drop in blood pressure, exacerbation of preexisting depressive symptoms.	A rebound rise in blood pressure may occur if the medication is rapidly discontinued.

S
E
C
T
I
O
N

III

Intervention:
A Treatment Perspective

S E C T I O N III

Intervention: A Treatment Perspective

CHAPTER 6

Approaches to the Psychosocial Treatment of Learning-Disabled Children Within a School Setting

E pidemiological studies estimate that the prevalence of children in the general population whose emotional difficulties require clinical attention is approximately 11.8 percent (Gould, Wunsch-Hitzig, & Dohrewend, 1981). As attested in previous chapters, learning-disabled children are at even greater risk to manifest problems at home, in school, and in the community that require intervention on some level. Unfortunately, treatment is often inadequate and fragmented. Problems are defined as "school problems" or as "family problems," for example, and solutions are parceled out among agencies, schools, and therapists without recognition of the interdependence of the problems (for a full discussion of this issue, see Chapter 7). A premise of this chapter, then, is that an efficient psychosocial intervention is based primarily on child and family needs, rather than on agency (or school) features and limitations, and that service components (mental health clinic, school, social service department, juvenile services) would reduce their workload by creatively altering and coordinating their services. For example, in a suspected child abuse case the same school program might be more effective if embedded in a working relationship with social services such that a protective service worker, school guidance counselor, family, and if necessary, school principal, participate in the same family interviews.

With such a model of treatment assumed, this chapter will first address the treatment of learning-disabled children in the context of their most significant social system, the family. Two other treatment approaches currently utilized with learning-disabled children will then be reviewed briefly: teaching social skills to learning-disabled children, and as a variant of such direct interventions, cognitive-behavioral therapy, both of which are based on an appreciation of the importance of another significant social system of the child, his or her peers. Finally, the use of behavior management techniques within the classroom will be addressed. It should be noted that this chapter provides neither an exhaustively detailed nor a comprehensive critique of all available treatments of learning-disabled children with psychosocial problems. For example, a discussion of traditional, psychodynamic play therapy with children is excluded here (note that this form of therapy has been written about elsewhere, e.g., Moustakas, 1973). Rather, this chapter provides a glimpse of four approaches that have demonstrated some special clinical utility in the treatment of learning-disabled children within the school setting.

THERAPY WITH THE FAMILIES OF LEARNING-DISABLED CHILDREN

In a recent article, Wilchesky and Reynolds (1986) very elegantly described a family systems approach to the treatment of learning-disabled children. They first outlined etiological factors involved in the development of social interactional problems of learning-disabled children: (1) the secondary effect of school failure; (2) the basic psychological processing and/or expressive deficits; and (3) dysfunctional family systems. Wilchesky and Reynolds clearly rejected the notion that parents "cause" specific learning disabilities or their associated behavioral difficulties. However, based on several years of clinical exerience, they defined three broad categories of families seeking help with their learning-disabled children.

> *Category 1:* There is the "relatively well-functioning family who without the added stress of the LD child would be able to manage quite well."
> *Category 2:* There is the family for which the added stress of "an LD child may be enough to result in dysfunctional patterns of interactions when otherwise normal life events occur (e.g., an adolescent leaving home, a younger child beginning school, etc.)."

Category 3: There is the LD child who is born into an already dysfunctional family "characterized by overprotection, enmeshment, overinvolvement, an inability to solve conflicts, and a tendency to resort to old solutions to new problems" (p. 412).

In the second and third types of families, Wilchesky and Reynolds viewed the problems of the learning-disabled child and the extant family dynamic as interacting in such a way as to exacerbate the child's (and family's) problems. Chapter 3 contains a full discussion of the family relations of learning-disabled children.

The Initial Interview

Although this is not intended to serve as a treatment manual for the psychosocial problems of learning-disabled children, we recommend, consonant with Wilchesky and Reynolds (1986), an integrated treatment model that includes an initial interview of the learning-disabled child and his or her family. This might include extended family members as well, especially when grandparents or other family members are already integral to the child's problems and, thereby, integral to their solution. Such an arrangement is the ideal, of course, and cannot always be achieved for practical reasons (e.g., schools cannot usually provide evening appointments for working parents), or may be blocked by "professional resistance," as described later in this chapter. However, the specific context surrounding a learning-disabled child's problems — for example, a very close and concerned mother and an underinvolved and seemingly uncaring father, or an overachieving sibling who shines by comparison to his or her learning-disabled brother or sister — can be assessed even when particular family members do not attend initial or follow-up interviews.

In fact, many family therapists routinely explore, with or without relevant family members present, the history of a particular person's functioning by discerning transgenerational patterns of familial behavior among grandparents, parents, and siblings of the child identified as the therapy client. This is not an endorsement for the more traditional approach within schools — for a counselor to treat learning-disabled children in isolation. Rather, it is recognition that individuals carry with them their family context or "process" which can serve as the focus of treatment regardless of who is in the therapy room. For example, learning-disabled children may have integrated the concept that they are worthless, and most probably, that they are at fault, because they cannot read. Their fathers may also feel inadequate with regard to their own school experiences and may be overly sensitive to how their children's poor school performance reflects on them.

In such a situation, fathers may convince their learning-disabled children by their hypercriticism that an inability to read makes the children "dumb." A more dramatic illustration of how children integrate family "injunctions" or commands has been described elsewhere by Kalof (1987), who reported that adults who were sexually abused as children or teenagers often have accepted, with or without their awareness, a variety of family commandments or rules. They might believe or behave as if they believe that "it is not OK to feel" or that "to be a good girl is to be a bad girl." Similarly, a learning-disabled child may have integrated or "owned" various family messages — for example, that because successful experiences in school have been infrequent for men in a particular family, and seem improbable in the future, they are not to be pursued. Instead, it is most important to appear physically threatening or "tough," and to defend one's worth by fighting with peers or by engaging in verbal altercations with teachers. This might be described as the "might makes right for past defeats" injunction. How such familial themes can be addressed in treatment is a subtle process, more easily understood through observation than description, and may be beyond the ken of this chapter. Clearly, there are no therapeutic prescriptions universally applicable to all families with a child presenting a particular kind of problem (e.g., underachievement in school, suicidal behavior, or school refusal). Nonetheless, without an initial family interview — a picture of the family in action — it is more difficult and may take longer to understand the symptoms of the learning-disabled child and what they mean. Without the family in the therapy room, it is impossible to alter familial patterns, perceptions, or experiences, and attempts to mediate the experience or perceptions of the learning-disabled child are rendered less powerful.

This approach presents a somewhat radical departure for schools. Involvement in family oriented therapy has not traditionally been something with which the education agencies have been comfortable.

An Underlying Philosophy to Promote Functional Interaction

Most often families with children "in trouble" feel blamed and disenfranchised, and as a result, they "resist" the best efforts of helpers — principals, therapists, counselors, parole agents, and others. Resistance is not all bad — it represents energy (e.g., to be a careful consumer of mental health services and to critically consider their utility), which, if handled correctly, can be utilized in the pursuit of treatment goals. However, a more workable starting point, one that engenders no more resistance in the family than already exists, is based on the following assumption:

> That the child and his/her family have inherent strengths and competencies that are not being expressed in the present context, and that in altering the context by introducing more functional interactions among system members, the family will be empowered to deal with the present crisis and to cope with future crises. The discouragement and hopelessness that are characteristic of families in crisis are challenged by the therapist's "dreaming for" the child; expecting that change can occur, and that success and satisfaction are indeed possible. Understanding that the problem is an expression of dysfunction within the system, and that there are no victims or oppressors, precludes... "saving" the child from the family.... In all situations with the child, the family, and extrafamilial systems, the [therapist] needs to observe the competencies demonstrated, to avoid a problem focused orientation, and to "stroke" every bit of functional interaction that occurs. The experience of competence, especially when it is highlighted, acts to bring into awareness the strengths people have forgotten they have, and to move them to the hopeful and optimistic position that sets the stage for change. (Family Therapy Practice Center, (1983 p. ii-II)

One version (of many possible operationalizations) of this philosophy is presented in the following case study.

Case Study 7: The Mystery of the Underachieving Boy

Johnny, a 12 year old learning-disabled boy for whom severe organic and/or thought processing problems were ruled out, "played simple" (note that these were his words) with his single-parent mother by forgetting to do his chores, responding slowly, if at all, to her simple questions or requests, and consistently adopting a passive stance such that she literally "filled in the gaps" for him by answering her own questions of him, completing or giving up the chores he forgot, and assuming that he really had no homework or could not do it when he shrugged his shoulders in response to her queries. She was very close to her son, but was frustrated and perplexed by his behavior. Similarly, Johnny displayed enigmatic behavior at school, as when he brought a long metal pipe to the playground and threatened a boy who teased his sister. He rarely completed his school assignments, and managed to do just enough work to get by. Johnny had contact with the police for a shoplifting incident and on one occasion failed to give his name or address to the police when they stopped him on the street after dark.

Obviously, a variety of explanations of, and potential solutions for, Johnny's behavior could be offered. He could be described variously as deliquent, oppositional at home, underachieving at school (even for a boy with a learning disability), or possibly depressed, and therefore, as province for the valid concern of a juvenile corrections officer, a psychiatrist or other mental health worker, school counselor, or social service worker. Alternatively, and perhaps in a well-coordinated response with Johnny, his mother, the juvenile officer, and the school counselor as participants, Johnny's "cunning" could be acknowledged and his mother given credit for her sensitivity. Over an extended period of time, Johnny very ably got his mother and other adults to relieve him of the common and ordinary responsibilities of a 12 year old boy by pretending to be mysteriously simple until they finally believed him, or at least, acted as if they believed him. Perhaps as a initial step, his mother could be given the opportunity, as the head of this single parent family, to describe what changes in Johnny's behavior would indicate satisfactory change to her — must Johnny become a straight-A student, or would passing three out of four subjects do? Her permissiveness could be countered by asserting that she was giving her child the advantage of limit-setting, which would help him succeed in school. Once the problem is defined and all family members agree to the therapeutic contract and to a mutual promise of participation in achieving a set of goals, the first significant change has been made, especially if Johnny abandons his impassive stance and actively expresses his point of view. It is only after success in the session — an interactional sequence in which Johnny steps out of his passive role and Mother supports it — that the family is asked to do the task again (or in some altered form) at home. The therapist selects a task that the family is able to accomplish, and assures success within the session by coaching, encouraging, stopping the process when it reverts to an old pattern or "family dance," and getting change to occur in the present. Later, when Johnny takes age-appropriate responsibility for completing his homework, he is congratulated, as is his mother, who refrains from her usual rescuing behaviors. The family dance now has new steps.

Highlighting Competencies Within Therapy — Further Elaboration

As important as the relationship between the therapist and the individual learning-disabled client is, it is unlikely to match the importance of parental or sibling relationships. As stated in the previous section, it is assumed that the altered perception of a learning-disabled child by his parent — from one of disappointment to one that "frames" or defines the child more positively and perhaps even similarly to the parent in a variety of ways — appearance, motivation, loyalty, ability to persevere, hopelessness, genetic endowment, sensitivity to others' opinion, or strength of character — far outweighs the impact on the child of the therapist's support and endorsement. Additionally, the parents' perceptions of, and behaviors toward, their problematic child can be challenged only after the parents have experienced themselves as competent and not under attack, as when they are criticized directly or indirectly by the therapist. Even well-intentioned suggestions or problem solving by the therapist may function as or feel like criticism to the parents and make them less amenable to challenges to try something different, despite the fact that short-term gains for the child may have been produced. By validating that the child is the "victim" of poor parenting and that he or she can be more effective than the parents, the therapist will likely fail in the long run. Simple and seemingly magical removal of a child's symptomatic behavior without first empowering parents by making them instrumental in the change process can have dire consequences. Parents will often "fire" their therapist by not returning for more appointments, or they may sabotage treatment efforts in other ways. Many parents who approach mental health persons for help with their children feel very inadequate in their parenting role and hold the strong belief that they are singularly at fault for their child's problems. This is even more often the case when parents defensively attribute blame to other people (e.g., the teacher or principal) or other institutions or agencies (e.g., the school or the department of social services).

Case Study #8: The Know-It-All Family
    Mr. and Mrs. All had two sons — one who had been adopted and was subsequently placed with another adoptive family by the Alls, and a 7 year old birth son, Graham, who had severe and varied learning disabilities. The Alls were professionals who had very high expectations for their remaining son. They had pushed the school system very hard to obtain special services for him, but had alienated many administrators and teachers in the process. They often observed Graham in the classroom, and on one occasion went into the class to intervene directly with their child and his classmates during a transition period. They agreed to attend family interviews, but demanded that Graham's two teachers and the school principal participate as well. From the point of view of Mr. and Mrs. All, the therapist's role was ancillary to their role in instructing the school

staff as to the best techniques for dealing with Graham. Intermittent attempts by the staff or therapist to make helpful comments based on their teaching and clinical experience with Graham were dimissed by the Alls, who repeatedly expressed their opinion that Graham's intellectual or psychomotor abilities were being underestimated and underchallenged. Only when Mr. and Mrs. All were recognized as the "experts" on Graham and problem-solving attempts were abandoned by the staff, did a window of opportunity open, allowing for a feeling of safety and mutuality between the family and the school staff. Formality in the meetings was reduced (the Alls had preferred that everyone sit around a table, but gave up the idea when the therapist was adamant in changing the format), Graham was allowed to come in and out of the therapy room to play, and any opportunity for casual banter between parents and staff was capitalized on, such that the sessions were less pressured and lighter in tone. Graham's cuteness and minor accomplishments in the classroom were delighted in. With Mr. and Mrs. All (and the school staff) less on the defensive, the therapist revealed to the Alls that she understood how difficult it was to be an advocate for a child with so many needs, that she knew that they were motivated out of love for Graham, and that they wanted to be effective without "scaring-off" the very people from whom they were seeking assistance. Furthermore, the therapist defined the real challenge for the school and for Mr. and Mrs. All as getting unstuck from "us" against "them" triangles in which parents, teachers, principal, child, therapist, previous school staff, and Board of Education were pitted against one another. Although dramatic changes were not forthcoming, the Alls more willingly attended family sessions, and after noticing improvements in their son's school performance (due largely to the hard work of Graham's teachers and implementation of behavioral techniques in his classroom), Mr. and Mrs. All described the school as "the best Graham had ever attended." They also inquired (in a nonoffensive way) about Graham receiving individual counseling in addition to their participation in family interviews.

The underlying theme — or "basso profundo" — in work with families of learning-disabled children is first to positively connote, whenever possible, the attempts of parents and their children, within the session to relate to one another in a competent manner, and second, to do so outside the session. Obviously, one's ability to relate to parents and children in such a respectful (and therapeutic) manner will be bounded by one's attitudes toward and beliefs about families with children "in a tough spot" — doing poorly in school, having poor peer relationships, or whatever defines the referral problem.

As mentioned before it is only when parents are empowered by recognizing their own capabilities that challenges can be issued to attempt something different, and it is hoped, more effective in dealing with their child. Such a challenge might involve the simplest of gestures — getting parents to get their children to sit up in the interview, pay attention, and hold their comments until it is their turn to speak. Another kind of challenge might be getting parents to reassure their child that the parents can handle an impending divorce without falling apart and without the help of the child who is failing at school because he or she is staying home everyday. This might take place by having the parents describe areas of their own lives that were intact and about which they were feeling hopeful, rather than depressed or helpless. Again, the elevation in treatment of the learning-disabled child and his or her parents, who likely feel highly ineffectual to begin with, is a fundamental premise of any approach likely to be effective with learning-disabled children and their families.

Professional Problems in Working with Families of Learning-Disabled Children

As Wilchesky and Reynolds (1986) pointed out, there is sometimes professional resistance to treating the families of learning-disabled children. They identified the "professional investment" phenomenon as the tendency "for each professional discipline to perceive the entire problem through its own window of specialization" (p. 414) and as a result, they treat the learning-disabled child in isolation. This can be true with pediatricians, psychoeducational consultants, perceptual-motor therapists, clinical psychologists, behavioral psychologists, or psychiatrists — just to name a few professional disciplines. Concomitantly, various professionals hold pet theories about the etiology of learning disabilities, which dictate their narrow approaches. Wilchesky and Reynolds (1986) advocated a "multicausal" explanation of learning disabilities which acknowledges some intra-individual variables that need to be addressed. Moreover, they "believe that many other inter-individual factors must be addressed in treatment" (p. 415) which require cooperative efforts by professionals who examine problems contextually, that is, within the family (and when the learning-disabled child is socially deficient, within the peer group).

A second problem, endemic to professional disciplines involved in the study and treatment of learning-disabled children, is a "perceptual disability" — the inability to see past the pathology that our particular window of specialization allows us to see. Various specialties are able to identify very specific (and important!) intraindividual deficiencies among learning-disabled children. This process allows the proper prescription of particular teaching techniques, for example, that help address the educational needs of the child. In other cases, very specific dispositions can be made based upon medical evaluations or psychological assessments. However, in the context of family treatment when a therapist is attempting to create a different, more competency-based experience for parents and child, one's ability to see beyond symptomatic behaviors (i.e., deficiencies) hinges on the ability to understand and identify with the family's ordeal, and to convincingly argue that "the glass is half full" — that although their child seems not to care about school, friends, or the family, for example, he or she is not a "bad" child but, perhaps, a child who missed a developmental step which was exacerbated by his or her learning disablilty — the child does not trust his or her own initiatives or attempts to positively affect the future. In the therapy room, this might translate into a boy's trust that he can speak for himself without yelling to be heard or to make a point. Emphasizing that the learning-disabled boy in this case has a speech dysfluency (a "stutter") might only hinder one's ability to "normalize" his attempts at communication, that is, to promote a more positive experience for the boy and his family. Unfortunately, what comes easiest for many professionals who work with disabled children and their families is the perception of inadequacies — an "enmeshed mother," a borderline retarded sibling, or an underachieving and depressed father. Although such data are crucial to keep in mind, the more difficult therapeutic task is to redefine such limitations in terms that facilitate mastery, rather than promote despair.

BEHAVIORAL TREATMENTS WITH LEARNING-DISABLED CHILDREN

Teaching Social Skills to Learning-Disabled Children in a Group

Controversy surrounding the issue of social competence in learning-disabled children was discussed earlier (see Chapter 3). Concomitant to research efforts identifying peer problems among learning-disabled children (e.g., Bryan, 1978), there have been investigations of attempts to remediate such problems through the promotion or direct teaching of a variety of very specific social skills (e.g., LaGreca & Mesibov, 1981; LaGreca & Santogrossi, 1980; Minskoff, 1980). Wilchesky and Reynolds (1986), for example asserted that "many socially deficient LD children require some form of peer group therapy to help them learn the social cognitive and behavioral skills to interact more adaptively with children their own age" (p. 414). Given a particular learning-disabled child's perceptual problems, such as an inability to accurately "read" nonverbal social cues (facial expressions, tone of voice, or body posture), Wilchesky and Reynolds argued that a peer group would provide the most appropriate context for learning and practicing such skills, especially if other systemic or family variables were addressed in additional meetings (e.g., other siblings' reactions to changes in the learning-disabled child). A different set of benefits to participation in group treatment would be accrued by a language-disabled child who misconstrued the content and intent of what peers said to him or her and then reacted to them impulsively and ineffectively. Wilchesky and Reynolds highlighted two additional group treatment goals that have particular relevancy for learning-disabled children — the development of efficient problem-solving strategies (to be discussed later in this chapter), and improved self-concept through the experience of more competent social interactions with group members.

Utilizing a very direct strategy, LaGreca and Mesibov (1981) successfully adapted to learning-disabled students a social intervention program developed to teach peer-interaction skills to nondisabled students, specifically a training program promoting "communication-conversational skills," and "taking the initiative in social situations." These skills were selected on the basis of LaGreca and Mesibov's (1979) previous work, which demonstrated that they contributed to a child's peer acceptance. Group sessions 60 minutes in length were held daily for 6 weeks of a summer school program with four learning-disabled students aged 12 to 16. Group procedures included modeling and coaching (e.g., discussions of how and when to use the skills) and behavioral rehearsal with feedback (e.g., videotaped practice of skills with peers). The group meetings focused on the following content areas: greeting skills (e.g., smiling and looking at a person and using their name), joining skills (e.g., approaching and greeting the person, asking to join and then following through, dealing with being turned down), conversational skills (e.g., speaking clearly, asking open-ended questions, sticking with the topic of conversation, and talking about personal subjects), and reviewing and practicing the skills identified. Group members' improvement was assessed using role plays of conversational skills and "talking in the halls," as well as raters' judgments of "skillfullness," comparing pre- and posttreatment assessments, as well as scores for learning-disabled students without social interaction problems. Overall, "the children who received treatment made consistent gains on measures of their conversation and joining skills, reported more frequent peer interactions, and were observed by others to develop improved interaction skills" (p. 199). LaGreca and Mesibov noted that these students still talked less than the normally interacting students during their roleplays, and ratings of their skillfulness were lower than those of the comparison students. Nontheless, such findings provide compelling evidence that such group social skills training may help remediate the peer problems of learning-disabled children.

An even more specific teaching approach for developing nonverbal communication skills in learning-disabled students with social perception deficits has been described by Minskoff (1980). She divided nonverbal communication skills into step-by-step sequences with a four-stage teaching approach: discrimination of specific social cues, understanding of the social meaning of such cues, appropriate usage of such cues, and application of such cues to actual social problems. Although Minskoff did not report an outcome study on the efficacy of the teaching activities she described, her study is ambitious (and unique) in its identification of accompanying methods and materials used in developing nonverbal communication skills involving body language cues. She suggested that Individual Educational Program (IEP) objectives for the development of social skills can be based on specific objectives, for example, teaching and assessing the discrimination of facial expressions, understanding their social meaning, meaningfully using facial expressions, and applying facial expression cues to communication situations in role plays. She outlined similar objectives in relation to nonverbal gestures and postures.

Each of the three group approaches to teaching social skills mentioned has merits that have not been fully or adequately tested with learning-disabled children. Nonetheless, they represent examples of attempts to intervene on a basic "skills-level," which contrasts sharply with the more global (and even less researched) familial approach to dealing with psychosocial problems of learning-disabled children described previously in this chapter.

Case Study #9: Steven, an 11 year old learning-disabled boy whose social skills were very poor, was reticent to speak, especially in a group context with his peers (he attended a school for learning disabled children). Social status was not measured in any systematic fashion (e.g., using sociometric nominations), but Steven was likely not very popular with his classmates. He had no good male friends. Steven's lack of social grace or assertiveness was demonstrated dramatically in one incident in which a classmate feigned anger toward Steven and pretended to be ready to throw a punch. Lacking the wherewithal to accurately estimate the seriousness of the situation and "bluff" or joke his way out of it (and thus maintain some status), Steven lunged at the other boy, and was subsequently pushed, falling to the floor and breaking his arm. Conversely, in other one-to-one social interactions, Steven verbally overwhelmed his peers by speaking tangentially about computers or robotics, for example. Steven participated for 2 school years in a very behaviorally oriented social skills group with several boys, equally dysfunctional in thier social interactions. Tokens were rewarded to each boy and to the group as a whole, based on compliance with common "group rules" (e.g., no fighting, one person speaking at a time, no leaving the group room, listening when another person speaks). Individuals in the group also had specific target behaviors for which they were rewarded tokens as they displayed the behaviors. Tokens were reimbursable at the end of the group therapy hour (or could be saved over time) for snack foods and various other privileges (e.g., time on a video game, viewing videotapes of the group's role plays, or having lunch with one of the group leaders or members). Steven's individual target behaviors were speaking up, staying on topic, and showing others that he understood what they were saying (by connecting his statements with something they said). The group was structured so as to include a "talk time" for the initial 10 to 15 minutes, although it often extended to 20 or 30 minutes. During this time, group members were encouraged to bring up any individual concerns or issues about the group (e.g., conflicts with group members or leaders, setting up new rewards or target behaviors, planning how the group's time would be utilized). One routine group activity was role-plays or impromptu dramatic skits which were videotaped and later reviewed and critiqued by the group. Group members rotated roles in the skits and others were assigned to the jobs of director and camera person. Depending on the skill deficits of the member, the group leaders cast them in roles that would challenge their social compentencies by getting them to try something "out of character." For Steven, that meant taking on more assertive roles that required well-timed and focused verbalizations. For example, Steven was once cast in the role of a judge deliberating on a court case. He was forced to summarize the presentations of the two lawyers, and then express his decision. Such role-playing seemed to empower Steven and promoted his status within the group. Additionally, his awareness of the potential impact he had on others when his verbalizations were relevant and concise was elevated. Although a formal outcome study was not conducted (with pre- and postintervention measures, etc.), Steven was described by teachers as participating more actively in classroom discussions and activities as the year progressed.

Cognitive-Behavioral Treatment

Most types of cognitive-behavioral intervention with children involve "the training of thinking processes in order to modify child behaviour problems" (Kendall, 1984, p. 173). One example of cognitive-behavioral therapies for children is social cognition problem-solving training. This represents another effort to ameliorate the social dysfunctions of learning-disabled children and to improve their social competence. Cartledge and Milburn (1986) emphasized the importance of problem solving in the following way:

> Children, as well as adults, are constantly confronted with conflict situations that, depending on how apprpached, may either be resolved with little difficulty or could be exacerbated. It appears that one critical factor is problem-solving ability, since good problem solvers tend to evidence better social adjustment than those with limited skills in this area. (p. 108)

Cartledge and Milburn highlighted a problem-solving method for children, derived from one used with adults, which includes a four-part determination of (1) the problem, (2) alternative responses, (3) the appropriate solution, and (4) an evaluation. In the problem definition and formulation stage, a child's independent thinking style is developed by asking him or her questions that sensitize the child to feelings of being upset and when these feelings start; that determine the source of the feelings (i.e., what happened); and that determine what the child would have preferred to happen instead. In determining solutions, the child is helped to engender a variety of responses to the

problem behavior (e.g., another child takes his or her book) and consequences to these alternatives. Then such a list is prioritized by the
child and the most desirable solution is tried out first through role-
playing. The "trainer" or person assisting the child might demonstrate
how to enact the solution and the child then rehearses it before performing it in real life. Finally, the trainer facilitates an evaluation of
the solution by the child and other possible solutions are considered.

Cartledge and Milburn reviewed criticisms of such training for
children with language differences and learning-disabled children in
noting that language difficulties may interfere with such an approach
(Spivack & Shure, 1974). Spivack and Shure incorporated development
of vocabulary, word meaning, and language concepts, such as the
understanding of conditional if-then statements with such populations. Such training with linguistically different and language-disabled students may be best done in consultation with a language
specialist. In light of other research findings, Cartledge and Milburn
stated further that it might be necessary for trainers to minimize
aggressive, antisocial alternative solutions and maximize prosocial
solutions due to the tendency of such children to produce more
aggressive behavior alteratives. Even with difficulties related to the
specific application of problem-solving techniques to learning-disabled children, such techniques provide another piece in the arma-
ment for treating their psychosocial problems.

Case Study 10: Michael: The Scapegoat
    Michael was an angry 10 year old boy with poor
impulse control who was often "set-up" by classmates, and
as a result, he got into many fights. Michael's family was
highly dysfunctional — he was triangulated by very angry,
separating parents (each parent attempted to gain his
allegiance against the other parent). In the classroom,
Michael often tested the authority of his teachers, or
refused to work. A varigated treatment approach was adopted
for use with Michael, including couples therapy with his
parents, frequent use of time-out procedures in the classroom, and individual therapy sessions to promote his self-
control and to provide him with support in his very
difficult situation. Michael's sessions were styled after a
model developed by Kendall (1984). A variety of analogue
tasks were required of Michael, all of which involved
tolerance for frustration, planning, and so forth. Michael
was put on a "response-cost" reinforcement schedule
whereby he was given 20 tokens at the beginning of each

session. He lost tokens when he forgot to follow a pre-
scribed sequence of steps in approaching the task at hand
(participation in role plays, games, etc.). He could also win
bonus tokens for especially good thinking, patience, and
similar behaviors. Michael was highly invested in the token
system (and it was later adapted to his classroom). The
steps included the following: stopping to think; defining
what the problem was (e.g., choosing the best move in the
board game of Trouble); considering all his choices (e.g., the
variety of moves he could make); choosing an alternative;
evaluating the outcome (e.g., how his move turned out); and
making an appropriate coping statement (e.g., "It was a good
try, I'll try harder next time"). Michael's fighting behavior
was reduced as he learned more adaptive responses to the
set-ups of his peers, and he generally appeared less impulse-
ridden. However, his improvement was delimited by the ongoing family problems he was exposed to, and his parents'
unwillingness to address their problems in couples therapy.
Michael's prognosis was very poor and reflected the content
in which he found himself, rather than the efficacy of his
cognitive-behavioral treatment.

BEHAVIOR MANAGEMENT WITHIN THE CLASSROOM

The following section briefly discusses the implementation in
school of time-out procedures, token or point systems, and behavioral
contracting. Integrating such programs in schools is not without special administrative, training, instructional, and parental considerations, as highlighted by Cartledge and Milburn (1986) in the parallel
application of social skill instruction. They pointed out that the application of new techniques should be school-wide in order to ensure
that the same behaviors are being reinforced in the larger environment. School-wide application also ensures a predictability important
to the learning-disabled student's behavior. Administrators need to be
knowledgeable in ways to apply the techniques "in order to serve as
curriculm leaders" (p. 148). Most importantly, teachers need to be
encouraged and reinforced for providing appropriate management of
behavior in the classroom. Teachers' resistance is likely to relate to the
amount of time needed to plan and apply behavior management procedures, and reasonably so. For this reason, there needs to be a clear
rationale (such as prevention of more serious behavior management
problems) provided administratively to teachers and parents which

suggests full support for the extra work involved, at least initially, in applying new techniques. It cannot be assumed, however, that these skills will be in even the best teachers' repertoire. Therefore, a trained consultant should be available for "hands on" in-service and training of teachers in the implementation of such a system.

Central Ideas to the Use of Behavior Management Techniques

Operant Conditioning

Operant conditioning techniques involve "the assessment and modification of clearly defined overt behaviors that can be reliably recorded, and (includes) an emphasis on antecedent and consequent events to change behavior" (Kazdin, 1978, p. 549). An example of such overt behavior might be "out of seat behavior" by a student. The activating or antecedent event may have been the teacher putting a new assignment on the blackboard or another student verbally taunting the student whose behavior is being assessed and modified. The consequent event might involve the reaction of other students or the teacher to the misbehavior.

Time-out Procedure

Efforts to alter aggressive or disruptive behavior in the classroom involve the systematic removal of the peer group as a source of reinforcement. The time-out method is defined as "the response-contingent removal of the child who emits aggressive or disruptive behavior from the peer group . . . from the opportunity to obtain reinforcement, including the social reinforcement that may be forthcoming from peer attention" (Ross, 1978, p. 612). Ross asserted that there is convincing evidence with children that brief time-outs are more effective than longer periods of confinement. When time-outs are utilized in classrooms it often entails physically removing the child from the larger group. Physical struggles with out of control children should not be undertaken lightly. Staff must be trained in the proper way to avoid hurting the student, being hurt by the student, or escalating an already highly charged event. In individual work with children, a simple and effective modification of the techniques involves teacher and therapist merely turning their backs to the child, thus ignoring the inappropriate behavior.

Points or Tokens

The use of points or tokens was illustrated in Case Studies #9 and #10. Simply stated, disruptive or other negative behaviors in the classroom are modified by the contingent use of teacher attention and by delivery of tokens or points that are later exchanged for back-up reinforcers (Ross, 1978).

Behavior Contracting

Ross (1978) made the keen observation that "in day to day interactions of children with teachers, desirable behavior is all too often taken for granted, so that few if any consequences are forthcoming, whereas undesirable behavior . . . elicits all sorts of consequences" (p. 604). Therefore, it is necessary to establish written behavioral contracts between teacher and student that ensure the "scheduled exchange" of positive reinforcement between teacher and child. Any of a variety of contracts can be negotiated, for example, a teacher might attend to one student in particular for 2 minutes following 10 minutes of in-seat behavior.

SUMMARY

Several methods for intervention at the level of the school system for the remediation of the psychosocial problems of learning-disabled children have been described. Although behavioral and systems approaches were delineated separately, their practical applications are rarely so separate. In fact, Maher (1981) has generated an approach at the interface of behavioral and systems psychology, emphasizing systems-related behavioral outcome goals. Clearly, neither intrapersonal variables nor interpersonal variables should take precedence in the treatment of the learning-disabled child. Moreover, therapists, principals, teachers, and other helpers need to be concerned about system boundaries outside the schools for the welfare of the learning-disabled child to be best addressed. A discussion of that issue emerges in Chapter 7.

Coordinating Services to the Child and Family

*C*hildren spend approximately one-third of each day in school environments. It seems appropriate, therefore, for the school to act as the coordinating agency in tracking the various services needed and the multiple providers of those services to learning-disabled children and their families. Public Law 94–142 mandates a range of related services to be provided by schools, including many types of mental health services such as counseling, psychological services, and social work. The exact nature of these services and the extent to which they are therapeutic will vary greatly. Traditionally, schools have focused only on school-related behavior problems, leaving the broader family and emotional issues to outside agencies.

As reviewed in Chapter 2, the most frequent types of behavior problems learning-disabled students experience are those that are external in nature and bring them into conflict with their environment.

Aggression (physical and/or verbal), hyperactivity, inattention, impulsiveness — these are all problems quite familiar to special educators. But as discussed in Chapter 3, these overt behaviors often mask more serious and deep-seated emotional problems or may exist in consort with other personality disturbances. At the very least these behavioral manifestations predispose the learning-disabled child and family to a systems breakdown that will certainly extend beyond the immediate school environment. How far, then, should schools go in their outreach to families in the provision of mental health services? Adopting a systems approach, such as the one suggested in Chapter 6, requires the school to take on a new role: that of case manager or coordinator.

THE IMPORTANCE OF CASE MANAGEMENT

Any complex system requires one central person — an executor — to coordinate and manage the various pieces so that the system does not fragment. Just as the diagnosis of a learning disability requires an interdisciplinary approach, so too does the intervention. But as alluded to in Chapter 6, there may be multiple barriers to the interdisciplinary cooperative process. Whereas Chapter 6 discussed the "window of specialization" effect encountered when different professionals view the same problem, this section will highlight other potential pitfalls and obstacles.

The Role of Case Manager

Researchers and practitioners agree that successful programs for learning-disabled students are facilitated by a case manager — an individual who coordinates and continuously monitors specialized treatments. Typically, the case manager's role is to oversee the implementation of program recommendations from the early phases of identification through intervention and program completion. The manager also serves as a liaison among the many parties involved in the provision of services: teachers, specialists, parents, etc. The communication among these individuals is enhanced since there is one central person charged with coordinating all facets of the educational plan.

In addition to maintenance of communication, it is the case manager's responsibility to ensure that services are provided in a timely manner and, when necessary, to request changes in the student's program. Finally, it is the case manager's responsibility to respond to the concerns and questions of parents, and to provide programming enabling parents to effectively deal with their children's problems.

Who's In Charge?

How is it decided who the case manager should be? The *psychologist* who provides therapy to the student and consultation to the teachers? The *social worker* who is in regular contact with the family and outside agencies? The *administrator* who ensures that the related services are available and provided in accordance with the IEP? The *principal* who is responsible for the day-to-day program? The *teacher* who depends on all these other people, but yet has the major responsibility of making it all work?

There are many sound reasons for choosing any one of these professionals to be case manager and that choice is best done when the student first enters the program. What is important is that the case manager have the time to follow the case appropriately and that he or she be able to communicate across discipline lines and understand each other's professional window of specialization.

Can the Team Work Together?

Facilitating interdisciplinary cooperation is often a difficult task as there are multiple barriers to overcome. The following is but a sampling of obstacles that must be dealt with:

1. Team leadership
2. Team trust
3. Professional turf guarding
4. Use of professional jargon
5. Professional competition

Each obstacle in its own way can determine the efforts of the team to appropriately implement the program.

Team Leadership

In a clinical, medical setting the team leader is almost always a physician. This is not the case, however, in a school setting where the leader is more likely to be the principal or other administrator. Whichever the case, the leader must be knowledgeable about each member's role and be able to facilitate cooperation and move the team along, overcoming other obstacles. The team leader sets the tone, keeps the team on track, and ensures that the team's work is completed.

Team Trust

In order for a team to develop a sense of trust in each other, each member's contribution must be valued. This sense of trust develops over time as the team works through other obstacles to interdisciplinary cooperation. Team trust can be fostered by each member asking sound questions to expand their knowledge base. In this way, the team meeting becomes an inservice training ground for all disciplines involved.

Professional Turf Guarding

This behavior involves the belief that no professional outside one's own discipline can adequately understand the importance of a relevant contribution to be made by the discipline. This "guarding of turf" undermines the team's efforts by keeping each professional separate and on guard that someone else will make a more important contribution or have a greater insight into the problems of the case. Turf guarders are generally invested in maintaining some predetermined professional hierarchy which prevents true communication from occurring.

Use of Jargon

The use of professional jargon ensures that the turf guarding will continue. As long as there are set phrases or terms to rely on, no one has to assume the responsibility for fostering the team's understanding of what is relevant from a particular window of specialization.

Professional Competition

This obstacle involves the belief that "my discipline is the most important one because it understands best the nature of the problem." As long as each team member is competing for a position of power, the team cannot work together.

Once leadership has been determined and trust established, the other obstacles can be overcome. The team is now ready to function as a unit and attempt to involve the outside agencies and multiple care givers involved in the case.

MULTIPLE CARE GIVERS

Some family systems are so complex and dysfunctional that a student brings with him or her multiple sources of services — that is, a protective service worker, a counselor from one or more community mental health centers, several medical clinic personnel, and so forth.

This may be the result of a family's shopping around for a particular service, such as medication, or the result of total dysfunction leading to involvement with many agencies. Whatever the cause, the result is one of the left hand not knowing what the right hand is doing. An example of this is clearly shown by the following case study.

Case Study #11: The Taylor Family

George Taylor, an 11 year old boy, was referred to a program for children with learning disabilities and began his new school at the beginning of the year. During the first weeks of school, George arrived unkempt, dirty, and disheveled, with no lunch or lunch money, and often fell asleep at his desk. Mrs. Taylor was difficult to reach, as they had no telephone. After many attempts at written communication went unanswered, school personnel made a home visit. It was learned at that time that George was one of six children, all of whom were in special education programs. The Taylor family was being seen sporadically by three different pediatric clinics, each prescribing medication for a different youngster. Mrs. Taylor had difficulty keeping straight whose prescription was whose. Additionally, three different mental health centers were involved; one providing counseling to Mrs. Taylor, one to George, and a separate one focusing on family issues. Last, the department of social services was involved — but from two different perspectives. A protective service worker was tracking an open case of neglect, while a regular worker assisted Mrs. Taylor in obtaining food stamps. Unfortunately, none of these professionals communicated with each other either to coordinate duplicated services or to cooperate with each other. George's school decided to take on the role of case manager and sponsored a meeting, invited all the professionals, past and current, involved with the Taylor family. The goal of this meeting was to consolidate services and to determine which agency, preferably the school, would act as the case manager.

INTERAGENCY COLLABORATION

When so many outside agencies are involved with a family it is vital that they collaborate with each other. Lack of collaboration is usually the result of lack of communication. Many of the issues raised earlier in this chapter can either facilitate this collaboration or impede it.

Different state and local agencies operate under different guidelines, depending on what role that agency is charged with. It is important for school personnel to develop a thorough understanding of each agency's jurisdiction, funding, and availability of services. In that way, the school can access a range of services in the most efficient way possible and avoid the common fragmentation that usually results from multiple care givers.

In come cases, services may be available in several places, that is, within the school or at a community mental health center. The team must then decide on the best source of service for a given situation, but duplication of services should be avoided. Facilitating interagency collaboration can be accomplished over time by determining one or two key staff personnel at each agency with whom school personnel deal with on a regular basis. Knowing *who* to call and *what* to ask can cut through the usual "red tape" associated with state agencies.

LINKING THE HOME, SCHOOL, AND COMMUNITY

Chapters 3 and 6 discussed two important social systems of the child: the school and the family. The community offers yet a third system in which the child functions. Linking theses environments together can provide a comprehensive system for implementing goals and objectives in the social/emotional and academic areas. A learning-disabled student in need of social skills training can get direct instruction in such skills at school, have them reinforced at home, and practice them by joining a community activity such as scouting or little league. For schools to ignore such important linkages only fosters isolationism and narrows the arenas available to help the student. These liasons become most crucial as the learning-disabled student ages and moves toward the world of work.

THE IMPORTANCE OF PREVOCATIONAL AND VOCATIONAL PLANNING

Many families are finding out that after many years of special education, their learning-disabled child has earned enough "units" to graduate but is totally unprepared to hold down a job. Vocational training and career counseling are often completely ignored when developing a student's IEP. If attention is paid to this critical area, it is often too little and too late. Prevocational planning and training should begin in elementary school and sound vocational programs must be available from junior high school on. But more often than not, what the learning-disabled students find is that their academic and social problems prevent them from being accepted into the regular education vocational programs. They are, however, equally inappropriate for special education vocational training programs which traditionally have served intellectually limited populations.

Learning-disabled students often lack the necessary social skills to make it on the job. They are capable of learning the basic job skill required but may have problems getting along with authority figures and co-workers. Time spent directly involved with the job may be successful, but the less-structured atmosphere of coffee breaks or lunch may become trouble spots. Curriculum planning should include, as part of social skills training, direct instruction in use of leisure time.

SUMMARY

It has been demonstrated throughout the preceding chapters that learning disabled students are at great risk for developing behavioral and emotional problems which will likely interfere with classroom performance. Because of the similarities in both learning disabled and emotionally disturbed students, teachers much be knowledgeable and adequately trained in remedial instruction, traditionally reserved for the learning disabled, and in those psychotherapeutic classroom techniques used in classes for the emotionally disturbed.

The overrriding conclusion of this text should be the importance of using a multidisciplinary team approach in providing services to learning disabled children with behavioral problems. The team, if functioning well, will support its member while adding multiple viewpoints and perspectives for consideration.

The linkages established by the team will determine the degree of success achieved in working with an individual child and family. Through linking the home, school, and community, a comprehensive plan will emerge that addresses the academic, social/emotional, and vocational needs of learning disabled students.

References

Alessi, N. E. (1984). Suicidal behavior among serious juvenile offenders. *American Journal of Psychiatry, 141,* 286–287.

Alley, G. R., Warner, M. M., Schumaker, J. B., Deshler, D. D., & Clark, F. L. (1980). An epidemiological study of learning disabled and low achieving adolescents in secondary schools: Behavioral and emotional status from the perspective of parents and teachers. (Report No. 16). Lawrence, KS: University of Kansas, Institute for Research in Learning Disabilities.

American Psychiatric Association. (1980). *Diagnostic and statistical manual of mental disorders* (3rd ed.). Washington, DC: Author.

Aponte, H. J. (1976). The family-school interview: An eco-structured approach. *Family Process, 15,* 303–311.

Becker, L. (1978). Learning characteristics of educationally handicapped and retarded children. *Exceptional Children, 44,* 502–511.

Berk, R. A. (1982). Effectiveness of discrepancy score methods for screening children with learning disabilities. *Learning Disabilities, 1,* 11–24.

Berk, R. A. (1983). The value of WISC-R profile analysis for the differential diagnosis of learning disabled children. *Journal of Clinical Psychology, 39,* 133–136.

Berk, R. A. (1984). *Screening and diagnosis of children with learning disabilities.* Springfield, IL: Charles C. Thomas.

Bonney, M. R. (1971). Assessment of efforts to aid socially isolated elementary school pupils. *Journal of Educational Research, 64,* 345–364.

Bower, E. M., & Lambert, N. M. (1965). In-school screening of children with emotional handicaps. In Long, N., Morse, W., & Newman, R. (Eds), *Conflict in the classroom* (pp. 128–129). CA: Wadsworth.

Bryan, J. H., Sherman, R., & Fisher, A. (1979). Learning disabled boys' nonverbal behaviors within a dyadic interview. *Learning Disability Quarterly, 1,* 65–72.

Bryan, T. (1982). Social skills of learning disabled children and youth: An overview. *Learning Disability Quarterly, 5,* 332–333.

Bryan, T., & Bryan, J. (1978). Social interactions of learning disabled children. *Learning Disability Quarterly, 1,* 33–38.

Bryan, T. H. (1974). Peer popularity of learning disabled children. *Journal of Learning Disabilities, 7,* 261–268.

Bryan, T. H. (1977). Learning disabled children's comprehension of nonverbal communication. *Journal of Learning Disabilities, 10,* 36–41.

Bryan, T. H. (1978). Social relationships and verbal interactions of learning disabled children. *Journal of Learning Disabilities, 11,* 107–115.

Bryan, T. H., Wheeler, R., Felcan, J., & Henek, T. (1976). "Come on dummy": An observational study of children's communications. *Journal of Learning Disabilities, 9,* 661–669.

Calhoun, G., & Elliott, R. (1977). Self concept and academic achievement of educable retarded and emotionally disturbed pupils. *Exceptional Children, 3,* 379–380.

Campbell, M. (1984). The use of lithium in children and adolescents. *Psychosomatics, 25,* 95–106.

Cantwell, D. P. (1972). Psychiatric illness in the families of hyperactive children. *Archives of General Psychiatry, 27,* 414–417.

Cantwell, D. P. (1975). *The hyperactive child.* New York: Spectrum Publications.

Cantwell, D. P. (1980). The diagnostic process and diagnostic classification in child psychiatry — DSM III. *Journal of the American Academy of Child Psychiatry, 19,* 345–355.

Cantwell, D. P. (1983). Depression in childhood: Clinical picture and diagnostic criteria. In D. P. Cantwell & G. A. Carlson (Eds.), *Affective Disorders in Childhood and Adolescence: An Update* (pp. 3–18). New York: Spectrum.

Cantwell, D. P. (1985). Organization and use of DSM-III. In D. Shaffer, A. A. Ehrhardt, & L. L. Greenhill, (Eds.), *The Clinical Guide to Child Psychiatry* (pp. 475–490). New York: The Free Press.

Cantwell, D. P. & Baker, L. (1980). Academic failures in children with communication disorders. *Journal of the American Academy of Child Psychiatry, 19,* 579–591.

Cantwell, D. P., & Forness, S. R. (1982). Learning disorders. *Journal of the American Academy of Child Psychiatry, 21,* 417–419.

Carlberg, C., & Kavale, K. (1980). The efficacy of special versus regular class placement for exceptional children: A meta analysis. *Learning Disability*

Quarterly, 14, 295–309.

Carlson, G. .A (1986). Classification of depression in children. In M. Rutter, C. E. Izzard, & P. B. Read (Eds.), *Depression in Young People: Developmental and Clinical Perspectives* (pp. 399–434). New York: Guilford Press.

Cartledge, G., & Milburn, J. F. (1986). *Teaching social skills to children.* Elmsford, NY: Pergamon Press.

Chandler, H. N., & Jones, K. (1983a). Learning disabled or emotionally disturbed: Does it make a difference? Part I. *Journal of Learning Disabilities, 16,* 432–434.

Chandler, H. N., & Jones, K. (1983b). Learning disabled or emotionally disturbed: Does it make a difference? Part II. *Journal of Learning Disabilities, 16,* 561–564.

Cohen, J. (1985). Learning disabilities and adolescence: Developmental considerations. *Adolescent Psychiatry, 12,* 177–196.

Colbert, P., Newman, B., Ney, P., & Young, J. (1982). Learning disabilities as a symptom of depression in children. *Journal of Learning Disabilities, 15,* 333–336.

Connors, C. K. (1969). A teacher rating scale for use in drug studies in children. *American Journal of Psychiatry, 126,* 884–888.

Cowen, E. L., Pederson, A., Babigian, H., Izzo, L. D., & Trost, M. A. (1973). Long-term follow-up of early detected vulnerable children. *Journal of Consulting and Clinical Psychology, 41,* 438–446.

Cullinan, D., Epstein, M. H., & Dembinski, R. J. (1979). Behavior problems of educationally handicapped and normal pupils. *Journal of Abnormal Psychology, 7,* 495–502.

Cullinan, D., Epstein, M., & Lloyd, J. W. (1983). *Behavior disorders of children and adolescents.* New Jersey: Prentice Hall.

Dean, R. (1978). Distinguishing learning disabled and emotionally disturbed children on the WISC-R. *Journal of Consulting and Clinical Psychology, 46,* 381–383.

Docherty, E. M., & Culbertson, W. C. (1982). The stability of child study team classification over four years. *Psychology in the Schools, 19,* 243–245.

Dudley-Marling, C. C., & Edmiaston, R. (1985). Social status of learning disabled children and adolescents: A review. *Learning Disability Quarterly, 8,* 189–204.

Earls, F. (1984). The epidemiology of depression in children and adolescents. *Pediatric Annals, 13,* 24–31.

Eisenberg, L. (1958). School phobia: A study in the communication of anxiety. *American Journal of Psychiatry, 114,* 712–718.

Eisenberg, L. (1959). The pediatric management of school phobia. *Journal of Pediatrics, 55,* 758–766.

Epstein, M. H., Bursuck, W., & Cullinan, D. (1985). Patterns of behavior problems among the learning disabled: Boys aged 12–18, girls aged 6–11 and girls aged 12–18. *Learning Disability Quarterly, 8*(2), 123–129.

Epstein, M. H., & Cullinan, D. (1983). Academic performance of behaviorally disordered and learning disabled pupils. *Journal of Special Education, 17,* 303–307.

Epstein, M., Cullinan, D., & Rosemier, R. (1983). Behavior problem patterns among the learning disabled: Boys aged 6–11. *Learning Disability Quarterly, 6*, 306–311.

Family Therapy Practice Center. (1983). *Single parent/adolescent foster care project.* Unpublished final report, Washington, DC.

Fish, M. C., & Jain, S. (1985). A systems approach in working with learning disabled children: Implications for school. *Journal of Learning Disabilities, 18*, 592–595.

Folstein, S. E. (1986). Emotional disorders in children. In G. Winokur & P. Clayton (Eds.), *The Medical Basis of Psychiatry* (pp. 352–366). Philadelphia: W. B. Saunders Co.

Folstein, S., & Rutter, M. (1977). Infantile autism: A genetic study of twenty-one twin pairs. *Journal of Child Psychology and Psychiatry, 18*, 297–321.

Forehand, R., Long, N., Brody, G. H., & Fauber, R. (1986). Home predictors of young adolescents' school behavior and academic performance. *Child Development, 57*, 1528–1533.

Forness, S., Bennett, L., & Tose, J. (1983). Academic deficits in emotionally disturbed children revisited. *Journal of the American Academy of Child Psychiatry, 22*, 140–144.

Forness, S. R., & Cantwell, D. P. (1982). DSM-III psychiatric diagnoses and special education categories. *Journal of Special Education, 16*, 49–63.

Forness, S. R., Sinclair, R., & Russell, A. T. (1984). Serving children with emotional disorders: Implications for educational policy. *American Journal of Orthopsychiatry, 54*, 22–32.

Friedrich, D., Fuller, G., & Davis, D. (1984). Learning disability: Fact or fiction. *Journal of Learning Disabilities, 17*, 205–209.

Furstenberg, F. F., Jr. (1985). Sociological ventures in child development. *Child Development, 56*, 281–288.

Gajar, A. (1979). Educable mentally retarded, learning disabled, emotionally disturbed: Similarities and differences. *Exceptional Children, 3*, 470–472.

Gajar, A. (1980). Characteristics across exceptional categories. *Journal of Special Education, 14*, 166–173.

Gallico, R. (1985). *The application of a discrepancy model with a cognitive behavioral profile for differentiating learning disabilities from emotional disturbance.* Ann Arbor, MI, University Microfilms International.

Ginsburg, M. M. (1985). *Processing deficits and social functioning of learning disabled children.* Unpublished doctoral dissertation, Catholic University of America, Washington, DC.

Gittelman, R. (1984). Anxiety disorders in children. *Psychiatry Update, 3*, 410–418.

Gittelman, R., & Klein, D. F. (1984). Relationahip between separation anxiety and panic and agoraphobic disorders. *Psychopathology, 17*, 56–65.

Glaser, K. (1968). Masked depression in children and adolescents. *Annual Progress in Child Psychiatry and Child Development, 1*, 345–355.

Glavin, J. P. (1974). Behaviorally oriented resource rooms: A follow-up. *Journal of Special Education, 8*, 337–347.

Glavin, J. P., & Annesley, F. R. (1971). Reading and arithmetic correlates of conduct-problem and withdrawn children. *Journal of Special Education, 5,* 213–219.

Glavin, J. P., Quay, H. C., & Werry, J. S. (1971). Behavioral and academic gains of conduct problem children in different classroom settings. *Exceptional Children, 2,* 441–446.

Goldfarb, W. (1980). Pervasive developmental disorder of childhood. In H. I. Kaplan, A. M. Freedman, & B. J. Sadock (Eds.), *Comprehensive textbook of psychiatry* (3rd ed, pp. 2527–2537). Baltimore: Williams & Wilkins.

Gottlieb, B. W., Gottlieb, J., Berkell, D., & Levy, L. (1986). Sociometric status and solitary play of LD boys and girls. *Journal of Learning Disabilities, 19,* 619–622.

Gottman, J., Gonsor, J., & Rasmussen, B. (1975). Social interaction, social competence, and friendship in children. *Child Development, 46,* 709–718.

Gottman, J. M., & Parkhurst, J. T. (1980). A developmental theory of friendship and acquaintanceship processes. In W. A. Collins (Ed.), *Minnesota symposia on child psychology* (Vol. 13, pp. 197–253). Hillsdale, NJ: Erlbaum.

Gould, M. S., Wunsch-Hitzig, R., & Dohrewend, B. (1981). Estimating the prevalence of childhood psychopathology. *Journal of the American Academy of Child Psychiatry, 20,* 462–476.

Graham, P., & Rutter, M. (1973). Psychiatric disorder in the young adolescent. *Proc. R. Soc. Med., 66,* 58.

Greenhill, L. L. (1985). The hyperkinetic syndrome. In D. Shaffer, A. A. Enhardt, & L. L. Greenhill (Eds.), *The clinical guide to child psychiatry* (pp. 251–275). New York: The Free Press.

Gresham, F. M., & Reschly, D. J. (1986). Social skills deficits and low peer acceptance of mainstreamed learning disabled children. *Learning Disability Quarterly, 9,* 23–32.

Grieger, R. M., & Richards, H. C. (1976). Prevalence and structure of behavior symptoms among children in special education and regular classroom settings. *Journal of School Psychology, 14,* 27–38.

Gualtieri, C. T., Koviath, U., & VanBourgondien, M. (1983). Learning disorders in children referred for psychiatric services. *Journal of American Academy of Child Psychiatry, 22,* 165–171.

Guze, S. B., & Robbins, E. (1970). Suicide and primary affective disorder. *British Journal of Psychiatry, 117,* 437–438.

Hallahan, D. P., & Kaufman, J. M. (1977). Labels, categories, behaviors: ED, LD, and EMR reconsidered. *Journal of Special Education, 11,* 139–149.

Harmon, R. J. (1982). Anaclitic depression: A follow-up from infancy to puberty. *Psychoanalytical Study of the Child, 37,* 67–94.

Harris, J., King, S. L., Reifler, J. P., & Rosenberg, L. A. (1984). Emotional and learning disorders in 6-12 year old boys attending special schools. *Journal of the American Academy of Child Psychiatry, 23,* 431–437.

Hartup, W. W. (1970). Peer interaction and social organization. In P. H. Mussen (Ed.), *Carmichael's manual of child psychology* (Vol. 2, 3rd ed.). NY: Wiley.

Hartup, W. W. (1981). Peer relations and family relations: Two social worlds. In M. Rutter (Ed.), *Scientific foundations of developmental psychiatry.* London: Heinemann Medical Books.

Hersov, L. A. (1960). Refusal to go to school. *Journal of Child Psychology and Psychiatry, 1,* 13–145.

Hess, R. D., & Holloway, S. D. (1984). Family and school as educational institutions. In R. D. Parke (Ed.), *The family* (pp. 179–222). Chicago: University of Chicago Press.

Hunt, R. D., & Cohen, D. J. (1984). Psychiatric aspects of learning difficulties. *Pediatric Clinics of North America, 31,* 471–497.

Jaffe, S. L., Magnuson, J. V. (1985). Anxiety disorders. In J. M. Wiener (Ed.), *Diagnosis and psychopharmacology of childhood and adolescent disorders* (pp. 199–214). NY: John Wiley & Sons.

Jain, S., & Zimmerman, B. J. (1984). *The learning disabled child and the family.* Unpublished manuscript. Graduate Center of the City University of New York.

Jary, M. L., & Stewart, M. A. (1985). Psychiatric disorder in the parents of adopted children with aggressive conduct disorder. *Neuropsychology, 13,* 7.

Kanner, L. (1943). Autistic disturbance of affective contact. *Nervous Child, 2,* 217–250.

Kaufman, A. S. (1976a). A new approach to the interpretation of test scatter in the WISC-R. *Journal of Learning Disabilities, 9,* 33–41.

Kaufman, A. S. (1976b). Verbal-performance I.Q. discrepancies on the WISC-R. *Journal of Consulting and Clinical Psychology, 44,* 739–744.

Kaufman, A. S., & Kaufman, N. L. (1983). *The Kaufman Assessment Battery for Children.* Circle Pines, NM: American Guidance Service.

Kaufman, J. (1982). Social policy issues in special education and related services for emotionally disturbed children and youth. In M. Noel & N. Haring (Eds.), *Progress of change: Issues in educating the emotionally disturbed: I. Identification and program planning.* Program Development Assistance System. University of Washington.

Kaufman, J. M. (1980). Where special education for disturbed children is going: A personal view. *Exceptional Children, 46,* 522–527.

Kazdin, A. E. (1978). The application of operant techniques in treatment, rehabilitation, and education. In S. L. Garfield & A. E. Bergin (Eds.), *Handbook of psychotherapy and behavior change.* New York: John Wiley & Sons.

Kellam, S. G., Ensminger, M. E., & Simon, M. B. (1980). Mental health in first grade and teenage drug, alcohol and cigarette use. *Drug Alcohol Dependence, 5,* 273.

Kendall, P. C. (1984). Annotation: Cognitive-behavioural self-control therapy for children. *Journal of Child Psychology and Psychiatry, 25,* 173–179.

Kendall, P. C., & Wilcox, L. E. (1979). Self-control in children: Development of a rating scale. *Journal of Consulting and Clinical Psychology, 47,* 1020–1029.

Kydd, R. R., & Werry, J. S. (1982). Schizophrenia in children under 16 years.

Journal of Autism and Developmental Disorder, 12, 343–358.

LaGreca, A., & Santogrossi, D. A. (1980). Social skills training with elementary school students: A behavioral group approach. *Journal of Consulting and Clinical Psychology, 45,* 220–227.

LaGreca, A. M., & Mesibov, G. B. (1981). Facilitating interpersonal functioning with peers in learning-disabled children. *Journal of Learning Disabilities, 14,* 197–240.

Lewis, D. O. (1985). Juvenile delinquency. In D. Shaffer, A. A. Ehrhardt, & L. L. Greenhill (Eds.), *The clinical guide to child psychiatry* (pp. 276–292). New York: The Free Press.

Lewis, D. O., Shanok, S. S., Pincus, J. H., & Glaser, G. H. (1979). Violent juvenile delinquents: Psychiatric, neurological, psychological and abuse factors. *Journal of the American Academy of Child Psychiatry, 18,* 307–319.

Loeber, R. (1983). Early predictors of male delinquency: A review. *Psychological Bulletin, 94,* 68–99.

MacDonald, K., & Parke, R. D. (1984). Bridging the gap: Parent-child play interaction and peer interactive competence. *Child Development, 55,* 1265–1277.

Maher, C. A. (1981). Intervention with school social systems: A behavioral-systems approach. *School Psychology Review, 10,* 490–508.

Mattison, R. E., Humphrey, F. J., Kales, S. N., Handford, H. A., Finkenbinder, R. L., & Hernit, R. C. (1986). Psychiatric background and diagnoses of children evaluated for special class placement. *Journal of the American Academy of Child Psychiatry, 25,* 514–520.

McCarthy, J. M., & Paraskevopoulos, J. (1969). Behavior patterns of learning disabled, emotionally disturbed and average children. *Exceptional Children, 10,* 69–74.

McConnaughty, S. H., & Ritter, D. (1985). Social competence and behavioral problems of learning disabled boys aged 6-11. *Journal of Learning Disabilities, 18*(9), 547–533.

McKinney, J. D., & Forman, S. G. (1982). Classroom behavior patterns of educable mentally handicapped, learning disabled, and emotionally handicapped students. *Journal of School Psychology, 20,* 271–279.

McLeod, J. (1983). Learning disability is for educators. *Annual Review of Learning Disabilities, 1,* 20–22.

Minskoff, E. H. (1980). Teaching approach for developing nonverbal communication skills in students with social perception deficits: Part I: The basic approach and body language clues. *Journal of Learning Disabilities, 13,* 9–14.

Minuchin, S. (1974). *Families and family therapy.* Cambridge, MA: Harvard University Press.

Morse, W. C., Cutler, R. L., & Fink, A. H. (1964). *Public school classes for the emotionally handicapped: A research analysis.* Washington, DC: The Council for Exceptional Children, NEA.

Motto, J. J., & Lathan, L. (1966). An analysis of children's educational achievement and related variables in a state psychiatric hospital. *Exceptional*

Children, 32, 619–623.

Moustakas, C. E. (1973). *Children in play therapy.* New York: J. Aronson.

Nichol, H. (1974). Children with learning disabilities referred to psychiatrists: A follow-up study. *Journal of Learning Disabilities, 7,* 118–122.

O'Donnell, D. J. (1985). Conduct disorders. In J. M. Weiner (Ed.), *Diagnosis and psychopharmacology of childhood and adolescent disorders* (pp. 249–283). New York: John Wiley & Sons.

Office of Special Education and Rehabilitation Services. (1986). *Eighth annual report to Congress on the implementation of Public Law 94-142: The education for all handicapped childrens act.* Washington, DC: U.S. Department of Education.

O'Grady, Dan. (1974). Psycholinguistic abilities in learning disabled, emotionally disturbed, and normal children. *Journal of Special Education, 8,* 157–165.

O'Quinn, A. N. (1985). Hyperactivity in children. In A. N. O'Quinn (Ed.), *Management of chronic disorders of childhood* (261–294). Boston: G. K. Hall Medical Publishers.

Ornitz, E. M., & Ritvo, E. R. (1976). The syndrome of autism: A critical review. *American Journal of Psychiatry, 133,* 609–621.

Perlmutter, B. F., Crocker, J., Cordray, D., & Garstecki, D. (1983). Sociometric status and related personality characteristics of mainstreamed learning disabled adolescents. *Learning Disability Quarterly, 6,* 20–30.

Pfeffer, C. R. (1986). *The suicidal child.* New York: Guilford Press.

Pfeffer, C. R., Conte, H. R., Plutchik, R., & Jerrett, I. (1980). Suicidal behavior in latency age children: An empirical study of an outpatient population. *Journal of the American Academy of Child Psychiatry, 19,* 703–710.

Pfeffer, C. R., Solomon, G., & Plutchik, R. (1982). Suicidal behavior in latency-age psychiatric inpatients. *Journal of the American Academy of Psychiatry, 21,* 564–569.

Pfeffer, C. R., Zuckerman, S., Plutchik, R., & Mizruchi, M. S. (1984). Suicidal behavior in normal school children: A comparison with child psychiatric inpatients. *Journal of the American Academy of Child Psychiatry, 23,* 416–423.

Phipps, R. (1982). The merging categories: Appropriate education or administrative convenience? *Journal of Learning Disabilities, 15,* 153–154.

Plas, J. M. (1986). *Systems psychology in the schools.* Elmsford, NY: Pergamon Press.

Poznanski, E. O. (1982). The clinical phenomenology of childhood depression. *American Journal of Orthopsychiatry, 52,* 308–313.

Puig-Antich, J. (1982). Major depression disorder and conduct disorder in prepuberty. *Journal of the American Academy of Child Psychiatry, 21,* 118–128.

Rapaport, J. L., & Ismond, D. R. (1984). *DSM-III training guide for diagnosis of childhood disorders.* New York: Brunner/Mazel.

Reynolds, C. R., Berk, R. A., Gutkin, T. B., Boodoo, G. M., Mann, L., Cox, J., Page, E. B., & Wilson, V. L. (1985). *Critical measurement issues in learning disabilities.* Report of the U.S. Department of Education, Special Education Programs Work Group on Measurement Issues in the Assessment of Learning Disabilities. Washington, DC: U.S. Department of Education.

Ricks, D. M., & Wing, L. (1976). Language communication and the use of symbols. In L. Wing (Ed.), *Early childhood autism* (pp. 93–134). Oxford: Pergamon Press.

Rie, H. E. (1966). Depression in childhood: A survey of some pertinent contributions. *Journal of the American Academy of Child Psychiatry, 5,* 653–685.

Roff, M. (1961). Childhood social interactions and young adult bad conduct. *Journal of Abnormal and Social Psychology, 63,* 333–337.

Roff, M., Sells, S. B., & Golden, M. M. (1972). *Social adjustment and personality development in children.* Minneapolis: University of Minnesota Press.

Rosenthal, P. A., & Rosenthal, S. (1984). Suicidal behavior by preschool children. *American Journal of Psychiatry, 141,* 520–525.

Ross, A. O. (1978). Behavior therapy with children. In S. L. Garfield & A. E. Bergin (Eds.), *Handbook of psychotherapy and behavior change.* New York: John Wiley & Sons.

Rutter, M. (1970). Autistic children: Infancy to adulthood. *Seminar Psychiatry, 2,* 245.

Rutter, M. (1974). Emotional disorders and underachievement. *Archives of Diseases of Childhood, 49,* 249–256.

Rutter, M. (1978). *Autism: A reappraisal of concepts and treatment.* New York: Plenum Press.

Rutter, M., Tizard, J., & Whitmore, K. (1970). *Education, health, and behavior.* London: Longman.

Rutter, M., Yule, B., Quinton, D., Rawlands, O., Yule, W., & Berger, M. (1974). Attainment and adjustment in two geographic areas: III. Some factors accounting for area differences. *British Journal of Psychiatry, 125,* 520–533.

Sabornie, E. J., & Kauffman, J. M. (1986). Social acceptance of learning disabled adolescents. *Learning Disability Quarterly, 9,* 55–60.

Shafii, M., Carrigan, S., Whittinghill, J. R., & Derrick, A. (1985). Psychological autopsy of completed suicide in children and adolescents. *American Journal of Psychiatry, 142,* 1061–1064.

Shaffer, D. (1978). "Soft" neurological signs and later psychiatric disorders: A review. *Journal of Child Psychology and Psychiatry, 19,* 63–66.

Shaffer, D., & Greenhill, L. (1979). A critical note on the predictive validity of the "hyperkinetic syndome." *Journal of Child Psychology and Psychiatry, 20,* 61–72.

Slate, J. R., & Sandargas, R. M. (1986). Differences in learning disabled and average students' classroom behaviors. *Learning Disability Quarterly, 9*(1), 61–67.

Soenksen, P. A., Flagg, C. L., & Schmits, D. W. (1981). Social communication in learning disabled students: A pragmatic analysis. *Journal of Learning Disabilities, 14,* 283–286.

Spivack, G., & Shure, M. B. (1974). *Social adjustment of young children.* San

Francisco, Jossey-Bass.

Spitz, R. (1946). Anaclitic depression. *Psychoanalytic study of the Child, 2,* 313–342.

Stewart, M. A. (1986). Conduct disorders and hyperactivity. In G. Winocur & P. Clayton (Eds.), *The medical basis of psychiatry* (pp. 285–307). Philadelphia: W. B. Saunders.

Stewart, M. A., & deBlois, C. S. (1985). Diagnostic criteria for aggressive conduct disorder. *Psychopathology, 18,* 11.

Stewart, M. A., deBlois, C. S., Meardon, J., & Cummings, C. (1980). Aggressive conduct disorder of children: The clinical picture. *Journal of Nervous and Mental Deficiency, 168,* 604.

Stone, F. B., & Rowley, V. N. (1964). Educational disability in emotionally disturbed children. *Exceptional Children, 5,* 423–426.

Sturge, C. (1982). Reading retardation and antisocial behavior. *Journal of Child Psychology and Psychiatry, 23,* 21–31.

Suomi, S. J. (1979). Peers, play, and primary prevention in primates. In M. W. Kent & J. E. Rolf (Eds.), *The primary prevention of psychopathology: Promoting social competence and coping in children.* Hanover, NH: University Press of New England.

Tamkin, A. S. (1960). A survey of educational disability in emotionally disturbed children. *Journal of Educational Research, 53,* 313–315.

The education of handicapped children, 34C.F.R.100, Implementation of Part B of the Education of the Handicapped Act, Department of Health Education and Welfare, Office of Education. Federal Register, (August 23, 1977).

Tsai, L. Y. (1986). Infantile autism and schizophrenia in childhood. In G. Winokur & P. Clayton (Eds.), *The medical basis of psychiatry* (pp. 331–351). Philadelphia: W. B. Saunders Co.

Ullman, C. A. (1957). Teachers, peers, and tests as predictors of adjustment. *Journal of Educational Psychology, 48,* 257–267.

U.S. Office of Education. (1977). Assistance to states for education for handicapped children: Procedures for evaluating specific learning disabilities. *Federal Register, 42*(250), 62082–62085.

Vance, B., Singer, M. G., Kitson, D. L., & Brenner, O. C. (1983). WISC-R profile analysis in differentiating LD from ED children. *Journal of Clinical Psychology, 39,* 125–132.

Webster, R. E., & Schenck, S. J. (1977). Diagnostic test pattern differences among learning disabled, emotionally disturbed, educable mentally retarded, and multi-handicapped students. *Journal of Educational Research, XX,* 75–80.

Weissman, M. D., Prusoff, B. A., & Gammon, G. D. (1984). Psychopathology in the children (ages 6-18) of depressed and normal parents. *Journal of the American Academy of Child Psychiatry, 23,* 78–84.

Werkman, S. (1980). Anxiety disorders. In H. I. Kaplan, A. M. Freedman, & B. J. Sadock (Eds.), *Comprehensive textbook of psychiatry* (3rd ed., pp. 2620–2631). Baltimore: Williams and Wilkins.

Werner, E. E., & Smith, R. S. (1982). *Vulnerable but invincible.* New York: McGraw-Hill.

Werner, M. A., Bryan, T., & Pearl, R. (1981). Learning disabled children's judgments of pro- and antisocial behaviors. Chicago, IL: University of Illinois at Chicago, Chicago Institute for the Study of Learning Disabilities.

Wilchesky, M., & Reynolds, T. (1986). The socially deficient LD child in context: A systems approach to assessment and treatment. *Journal of Learning Disabilities, 19,* 411–415.

Wright, L. S. (1984). Conduct problem or learning disability? *Journal of Special Education, 8,* 331–336.

Ysseldyke, J. E., & Algozzine, B. (1982). *Critical issues in special and remedial education.* Boston: Houghton Mifflin.

Ysseldyke, J. E., Algozinne, B., & Epps, S. (1983). A logical and empirical analysis of current practice in clarifying students as handicapped. *Exceptional Children, 50*(2), 160–166.

Ysseldyke, J. E., Algozzine, B., Shinn, M. R., & McGee, M. (1982). Similarities and differences between low achievers and students classified as learning disabled. *Journal of Special Education, 16,* 73–85.

Ysseldyke, J. E., & Foster, G. G. (1978). Bias in teachers observations of emotionally disturbed and learning disabled students. *Exceptional Children, 5,* 613–615.

Yule, W., & Rutter, M. (1985). Reading and other learning difficulties. In M. Rutter & L. Hersov (Eds.), *Child and adolescent psychiatry: Modern approaches* (pp. 444–462). St. Louis: Mosby.

Glossary

Ability-Achievement Discrepancy — a true or reliable difference between measured ability or IQ and measured achievement which is computed from the standard error of measurement of the difference between two test scores based on a statistical significance level equal to or less than 1 time out of 100 for a single analysis or 7 times out of 100 for a series of analyses.

Affect — outward expression of feeling, emotion, or mood.

Anaclitic — dependence of the infant on the mother (or mother substitute) for a sense of well-being.

Anaclitic Depression — profound disturbance of mood observed in young children deprived of early maternal attachment.

Anhedonia — inability to experience pleasure from activities that normally create a pleasurable response.

Antisocial Behavior — repeated conflicts with other individuals and groups. A limited capacity to abide by societal rules and norms.

Anxiety — anticipation of danger, often from unknown or unrecognized sources, which creates a state of tension, anticipation, and uneasiness.

Apathy — lack of interest and emotional connection to one's surroundings.

Attention Deficit Disorder — as defined by the DSM-III, a childhood psychiatric disturbance manifested by developmentally inappropriate poor attention span, impulsivity, and limited concentration. Often associated with motoric hyperactivity.

Brief Psychotic Reaction — state of severely disturbed reality orientation, clearly induced by environmental stressors, lasting for less than two weeks.

Bronchial Asthma — chronic and recurrent episodes of breathing difficulty due to temporary constriction of the bronchial passages (windpipes).

Catatonic — state marked by muscular rigidity, stupor, and negativism.

Cerebral Palsy — defect of motor power and coordination associated with brain damage, often caused by birth trauma.

Childhood Schizophrenia — schizophrenia occurring before puberty. Currently considered to occur very rarely. Many cases that in the past would have been considered to be childhood schizophrenia are, in the current DSM-III classification, more appropriately diagnosed as pervasive developmental disorders.

Compulsion — uncontrolled, insistent, repetitive, and unwanted urge to perform an act that is incompatible with one's normal behavior. The resistance to perform such an act leads to overt anxiety.

Cognitive — the act or process of knowing or the product of such knowledge; the various thinking skills such as comprehension, reasoning, and memory.

Conduct Disorder — by DSM-III nomenclature, a childhood psychiatric disorder marked by antisocial and aggressive behaviors.

Congenital Rubella — viral infection passed on from mother to fetus during intrauterine state, causing high incidence of severe abnormalities (especially of the brain) in affected children.

Cross-categorical — the grouping of different types of handicapped students (i.e., mentally retarded, learning disabled, emotionally disturbed) into one classroom.

Cytomegalovirus — viral infection with predilection for salivary glands, as well as passage from mother to in utero child with a high risk of fatal neonatal outcome.

Delusion — fixed, false belief that is held despite incontrovertible proof to the contrary.

Delusion of Control — false belief that thoughts, feelings, and actions are not one's own, but are imposed by some external force.

Depression — mental state marked by sadness, despair, discouragement, loneliness, guilt, and low self-esteem. Associated signs may include sleep and appetite disturbances, psychomotor agitation or psychomotor retardation, and low energy states.

Diabetes Mellitus — metabolic illness marked by deficiency of insulin (a pancreatic hormone necessary for utilization of carbohydrates). Serious complications may potentially occur in the peripheral nervous system, eyes, and kidneys.

Diagnostic and Statistical Manual, Third Revision (DSM-III) — standard classification of psychiatric disorders, first published by the American Psychiatric Association in 1980.

Diagnosis — determination of the nature of an illness or disorder, deduced by the examination of presenting signs and symptoms.

Differential Diagnosis — elucidation of two or more illnesses or disorders with signs and symptoms similar to the patient's clinical presentation.

Disciplinary Removal — action taken by the individual school as a consequence for a student's disruptive or aggressive behavior resulting in a temporary removal from school; usually not to exceed three days at one time.

Dysphoria — prevailing mood of depression, restlessness, and dissatisfaction.

Echolalia — meaningless repetition of overheard words or phrases.

Empathy — insightful and sensitive awareness and understanding of another person's state of mind.

Epidemiological — the science of studying factors affecting a large number of persons in a similar locality at the same time, allowing for the study of trends to occur.

Epidemiological Studies — studies that deal with the incidence, distribution, and control of disease or disorders in a population.

Etiology — the study of the cause of a condition.

Etiology or Etiological Factors — all the factors that contribute to the occurrence of a disease or abnormal condition.

Exclusionary Factors — those factors identified by Public Law 94-142 that must be ruled out before a diagnosis of learning disability or emotional disturbance can be made.

Externalizing Behaviors — those behaviors that have emerged as a broad band syndrome representing conflicts with the environment such as hyperactivity, aggressiveness, and deliquency.

Fragile X Syndrome — recent chromosomal finding, associated with expression of mental retardation and infantile autism.

Grandiose — exaggerated belief of one's own importance, often manifested by delusions of great power, fame, and wealth.

Hallucination — false sensory perception which occurs in the absence of any sensory stimulation; includes misperceptions in such senory modalities as auditory (hearing), visual (seeing), olfactory (smelling), gustatory (tasting), and tactile (touching).

Incoherence — communication that is disorganized, disconnected, and incomprehensible.

Infantile Autism — profound developmental disability caused by some as yet unknown brain abnormality. The disorder manifests during the first two and a half years of life and is marked by gross disturbance in language and social skills. Also known as "Kanner's Syndrome."

Interindividual Factors — contextual factors that influence (and are influenced by) the functioning of the individual (i.e., family functioning or sociometric status).

Interpersonal Bonding — attachment between two individuals whose identities are profoundly affected by their mutual interaction (i.e., the positive attachment often seen between a mother and her young child).

Internalizing Behaviors — those behaviors that have emerged as a broad band syndrome representing conflicts within oneself such as personality problems, depression, uncommunicativeness, obsessive-compulsiveness, somatic complaints, or immaturity.

Intraindividual Factors — psychological factors that exist or occur within the individual (e.g., basic psychological processing and/or expressive deficits).

In Utero — within the womb, the state prior to birth.

Lead Encephalopathy — seizures, delirium, hallucinations, and other signs of brain dysfunction precipitated by chronic lead poisoning.

Loosening of Associations — disturbance of thinking and speech manifested by illogical sequence and content; often seen in schizophrenic disorders.

Minimal Brain Dysfunction — descriptive term used prior to introduction of DSM-III classification; no longer in common use. Refers to a behavioral syndrome of childhood characterized by learning problems, distractability, poor attention span, hyperactivity, impulsivity, and emotional lability.

Morbid Ideation — thoughts focused on themes of suffering, illness, and death.

Morbidity Rate — proportion of individuals with a particular illness or disorder during a fixed period of time.

Mortality Rate — proportion of individuals who have died during a fixed period of time.

Multiaxial — a classification system used in the medical profession which allows for five multiple parallel diagnostic factors.

Mute — lacking the faculty for speech.

Neonatal — period of time immediately following birth and continuing through the first month of life.

Oppositional — behavior that is negativistic, disobedient, and provocative to authority.

Organic Brain Syndrome — mental disorders caused by transient or permanent brain dysfunction, attributable to a variety of specific organic factors.

Panic — overwhelming attacks of anxiety associated with a sense of impending doom. Physiological changes (including shortness of breath, palpitations, and gastrointestinal discomfort) are often associated.

Paranoid Ideation — severe suspiciousness or belief that one is being harrassed, persecuted, or unfairly treated; often achieving delusional proportions.

Perceptual — the product of the process of organizing or interpreting raw data obtained through the senses.

Perinatal — pertaining to the period of time directly before, during, and following the moment of birth.

Phenylketonuria (PKU) — inherited metabolic disease that causes mental retardation and seizures.

Predictive Validity — the accuracy of a test in predicting future learning problems.

Prenatal — preceding birth.

Profile Analysis — the examination of a set of scores from one test or multiple tests on the same individual.

Prognosis — forecasting of the probable outcome of an illness or disorder.

Psycholinguistics — the field of study that blends aspects of two disciplines — psychology and linguistics — to examine the total picture of the language process.

Psychomotor Agitation — generalized physical and emotional excitation and overactivity in response to external and/or internal stimuli.

Psychomotor Epilepsy — disorder characterized by impairment of conscious ness and amnesia for the episode, often associated with semipurposeful movements of the arms or legs and sometimes with perceptual disturbances (i.e., hallucinations).

Psychomotor Retardation — generalized physical and emotional slowing down in response to external and/or internal stimuli.

Psychopharmacology — study of the effects of psychoactive (or psychotropic) drugs on thinking, mood, and behavior.

Psychosis — severe mental disorder characterized by impairment in thinking, reality orientation, social relatedness, and emotional responsivity. The classical signs of psychosis are delusions, hallucinations, and illusions.

Reading Retardation — a term referring to students with specific disabilities in reading, resulting in a lag in their skills level.

Reality Testing — ability to objectively differentiate between the external world and the internal world.

Reliability — the degree of consistency between two or more measurements of the same thing.

Remediation — the correction of a defective or deficient skill.

Schizophrenia — psychotic mental disorder characterized by severe disturbances in thinking, mood, and behavior. Duration of disorder is longer than six months.

Schizophreniform Disorder — severe psychotic state lasting between two weeks and six months.

School Phobia — intense fear and refusal to attend school exhibited by children. Usually a manifestation of separation anxiety.

Self-esteem — conception of one's own identity, personality, and value as a person.

Separation Anxiety — fear and apprehension normally observed in infants when removed from their mothers (or mother substitutes). Considered to be pathological if experienced to a marked degree in later childhood.

Sign — objective abnormality indicative of an underlying illness or disorder.

Sociometric Status — a child's popularity among his or her peers as assessed through the application of quantitative methods to the study of the psychological properties of populations (e.g., a group of classmates). A wide variety of sociometric devices have been employed with children, but there are three major types: peer nominations, rating scales, and descriptive matching. Peer nominations require children to nominate their peers for inclusion into some imminent or purely hypothetical group. A variant of this approach requires children to chose others whom they simply like most and least. Rating scales ask children to rate each of their peers on some dimension of acceptability. Descriptive matching requires children to match up peers with various behavioral or personality descriptors.

Somatic — relating to the body.

Specific Developmental Disorders — according to the DSM-III, the areas of specific learning disability, including dysfunction in reading, arithmetic, and language.

Symptom — subjective perception of abnormal function or sensation.

Thought Broadcasting — delusional conviction that one's thoughts are being broadcast or projected into the environment (seen in schizophrenia).

Time Out — the removal of a student from all positive reinforcement such as attention or praise.

Toxoplasmosis — parasitic infection with predilection for brain and eyes. If passed from mother to in utero child, severe risk of prenatal death or severe brain and eye damage.

Validity — the accuracy of the intent or purposes for which a test is designed and the scores used.

Verbal-Performance Discrepancy — a true and reliable difference between the verbal portion and the performance portion of the WISC-R intelligence test.

Tests Commonly Used in Research and Diagnosis of Learning Disabilities and Emotional Disturbance

TESTS OF COGNITIVE ABILITY

Test	Publisher/Address
California Short Form Test of Mental Maturity	CTB/McGraw Hill Del Monte Research Park Monterey, CA 93940
Graham-Kendall Memory for Designs	Psychological Test Specialists Box 9229 Missoula, MT 59807
Kaufman Assessment Battery for Children (K-ABC)	American Guidance Service Publisher's Building Circle Pines, MN 55014
Stanford-Binet Intelligence Scale	The Riverside Publishing Co. 8420 Bryn Mawr Avenue Chicago, IL 60631

TESTS OF COGNITIVE ABILITY
(continued)

Test	Publisher/Address
Wechsler Intelligence Scale for Children (WISC) Wechsler Intelligence Scale for Children-Revised (WISC-R)	Psychological Corporation 7500 Old Oak Boulevard Cleveland, OH 44130

TESTS OF ACHIEVEMENT/PROCESSING

Test	Publisher/Address
California Achievement Test (CAT)	CTB/McGraw Hill Del Monte Research Park Monterey, CA 93940
Comprehensive Test of Basic Skills (CTBS)	CTB/McGraw Hill Del Monte Research Park Monterey, CA 93940
Gilmore Oral Reading Test	The Psychological Corporation 7500 Old Oak Boulevard Cleveland, OH 44130
Illinois Test of Psycholinguistic Abilities (ITPA)	Western Psychological Services 12031 Wilshire Boulevard Los Angeles, CA 90025
Iowa Test of Basic Skills	The Riverside Publishing Company 8420 Bryn Mawr Avenue Chicago, IL 60631
Stanford Achievement Tests	The Psychological Corporation 7500 Old Oak Boulevard Cleveland, OH 44130
Wepman Auditory Discrimination Test	Western Psychological Services 12031 Wilshire Boulevard Los Angeles, CA 90025
Wide Range Achievement Test (WRAT)	Guidance Associates of Delaware, Inc. 1526 Gilpin Avenue Wilmington, DE 19806

Test	Publisher/Address
Woodcock-Johnson Psychoeducational Battery	Teaching Resources Corp. 50 Pond Park Road Hingham, MA 02043

MEASURES OF BEHAVIOR

Test	Publisher/Address
Behavior Problems Checklist (BPC) Behavior Problems Checklist-Revised	Herbert C. Quay Univeristy of Miami Applied Social Sciences P.O. Box 248074 Coral Gables, FL 33124
Child Behavior Checklist	Thomas M. Achenbach Department of Psychiatry University of Vermont Burlington, VT 05401
Connors Teacher's Questionnaire	K. Connors Children's Hospital National Medical Center 111 Michigan Avenue, N.W. Washington, DC 20010
Childhood Self-Control Inventory	P.C. Kendall Department of Psychology Temple University Philadelphia, PA 19122

DSM-III-R

The Diagnostic and Statistical Manual, Third Edition, Revised (DSM-III-R) was published in May, 1987. Although the intended purpose of this revision is to improve diagnostic reliability, formal clinical reserach validation must still await future studies.

Since its original release in 1980, the DSM-III has achieved widespread success in standardizing psychiatric diagnosis. As the DSM-IV is not scheduled for publication until the early 1990s, some revision of established DSM-III diagnostic criteria has been considered desirable by many mental health researchers and practitioners. However, alteration of previously well-validated diagnostic criteria will not meet with immediate and universal acceptance. Particularly with the diagnoses relevant to child psychiatric disorders, resistance is to be expected. Consequently, for an appreciable period of time, professionals in the fields of mental health and education will most likely witness the application of both DSM-III and DSM-III-R criteria. It remains to be seen whether, in fact, DSM-III-R criteria will achieve greater usuage than DSM-III.

It is important for educators to be knowledgeable of the new and, as yet, unvalidated DSM-III-R criteria, as well as the standardized DSM-III perspective. A brief review of DSM-III-R criteria will be provided for those psychiatric disorders of children and adolescents which are discussed in the DSM-III paradigm in Chapter 4.

I. Autistic Disorder

The DSM-III-R considers autistic disorders to be a manifestation of the more generalized category of pervasive developmental disorder. Diagnostic criteria are divided into three categories: impairment in social interaction, impairment in communication, and restricted variety of activities and interests. Sixteen separate clinical signs and symptoms are subsumed within these three categories. In order to establish a diagnosis of autistic disorder, 8 of the overall 16 criteria must be present.

Impairment in social interaction — must include two of the following five items: incapacity to establish meaningful friendships and relationships; inability to engage in normal socialized play; inability to engage in healthy imitative behaviors; not directed to seek comfort when in distress; inability to conceptualize the feelings of others.

Impaired communication, both verbal and nonverbal — must include at least one of the following items: Total lack of meaningful communication, both verbal and nonverbal; lack of meaningful nonverbal communication; incapacity to utilize imagination; marked impairment and peculiarities in the production of speech; marked impairment and peculiarities in the content of speech; inability to initiate and maintain normal conversation in spite of adequate speech mechanisms.

Restricted variety of activities and interests — must include at least one of the following five items: severely narrow range of interests and perseverative preoccupation with one particular interest; insistence upon doing things in the same manner at all times; resistance to change in the environment, often of trival degree; persistent attachment to unusual objects; oddities of motor movement, in particular, stereotypies.

The category of autistic disorder distinguishes between infant and childhood onset by the critical point of 3 years of age.

II. Attention Deficit Disorder with Hyperactivity

The establishment of such a diagnosis occurs when a child's or adolescent's behavior is noticeably different when compared to others of the same mental age. By DSM-III-R criteria, a minimum time period of six months is required in order to establish the diagnosis.

In order to establish the diagnosis of attention deficit disorder with hyperactivity (ADDH), at least 8 of the following 14 signs and symptoms must be required: excessively fidgety; marked inability to remain in a required seated position; easily distracted by external stimuli; unable to await turn and abide by rules in group games; frequent yelling out answer to question prior to completion of stated question; inability to follow through on assignments and difficulty with instructions; poor capacity to sustain attention in either work or play context; frequent shifting from one activity to another; poor capacity to play quietly; excessive talking; frequent interruptions of others; often does not seem to listen; frequent loss of items that are important for tasks at home or school; poor judgment in evidence with frequent participation in potentially physically dangerous activities.

III. Conduct Disorder

Such behavior must be of at least six months' duration, and include 3 of the following 13 items: stealing not involving confrontation with a victim; running away from home overnight on at least two occasions; persistent serious lying; deliberate fire setting; frequent school truancy; destruction of other's property; forced entry into home or vehicle of another; utilization of force to engage in sexual activity with a nonconsenting other; frequently engaging in and initiating physical fights; theft involving the physical confrontation with a victim; deliberate cruelty to other individuals.

Subtypes of conduct disorder include the "group type," with signs and symptoms consistent with conduct disorder present only when in the company of others engaged in similar behavior; the "solitary aggressive type," with predominantly physically aggressive behavior initiated by the patient and directed toward others.

IV. Oppositional Defiant Disorder

Standardized according to mental age, the disturbance must be present for at least six months and subsume at least five of the following nine items: frequent usage of obscene language; vindictive and spiteful behavior; frequent anger and resentment; heightened irritability and annoyance when in the presence of others; tendency to blame others instead of assuming personal responsibility; deliberately provocative toward others; frequently defiant of socially acceptable rules and norms; argumentative with adults; frequent display of "temper."

V. Separation Anxiety Disorder

Marked by excessive anxiety focused upon a real or imagined separation from an important other, three of the following nine items must be present for at least two weeks in order to fulfill diagnostic criteria: excessive or unrealistic anxiety that harm will occur to a significant other; excessive and unrealistic anxiety that some natural or manmade catastrophe will separate the child from the significant other; persistent refusal to attent school in order to remain at home with primary attachment person; excessive clinging to major attachment figure and avoidance of being left alone; frequent nightmares involving separation themes; frequent physiological complants (i.e., headaches, stomachaches, nausea) when such problems might relieve the child from the responsibility of going to school; great anticipation and anxiety regarding possible future separations from major attachment figure: when actually separated from major attachment figure, expressing pervasive and nonremitting distress.

Behavioral Checklists Commonly Used with Learning-Disabled/Emotionally Disturbed Students

CHILDREN'S HOSPITAL NATIONAL MEDICAL CENTER
111 Michigan Avenue, N. W.
Washington, D. C. 20010

Teacher's Questionnaire

Name of Child _____   Grade _____

Date of Evaluation _____

Please answer all questions. Beside *each* item, indicate the degree
of the problem by a check mark (✔)

		Not at all	Just a little	Pretty much	Very much
1.	Restless in the "squirmy" sense.				
2.	Makes inappropriate noises when he shouldn't.				
3.	Demands must be met immediately.				
4.	Acts "smart" (impudent or sassy).				
5.	Temper outbursts and unpredictable behavior.				
6.	Overly sensitive to criticism.				
7.	Distractibility or attention span a problem.				
8.	Disturbs other children.				
9.	Daydreams.				
10.	Pouts and sulks.				
11.	Mood changes quickly and drastically.				
12.	Quarrelsome.				
13.	Submissive attitude toward authority.				
14.	Restless, always "up and on the go."				
15.	Excitable, impulsive.				
16.	Excessive demands for teacher's attention.				
17.	Appears to be unaccepted by group.				
18.	Appears to be easily led by other children.				
19.	No sense of fair play.				
20.	Appears to lack leadership.				
21.	Fails to finish things that he starts.				
22.	Childish and immature.				
23.	Denies mistakes or blames others.				
24.	Does not get along well with other children.				
25.	Uncooperative with classmates.				
26.	Easily frustrated in efforts.				
27.	Uncooperative with teacher.				
28.	Difficulty in learning.				

SELF-CONTROL IN CHILDREN RATING SCALE

Name of Child _____   Grade _____

Rater _____

Please rate this child according to the descriptions below by circling the appropriate number. The underlined 4 in the center of each row represents where the average child would fall on this item. Please do not hesitate to use the entire range of possible ratings.

1. When the child promises to do something, can you count on him or her to do it?

   1　2　3　4　5　6　7
   always　　　　never

2. Does the child butt into games or activities even when he or she hasn't been invited?

   1　2　3　4　5　6　7
   always　　　　never

3. Can the child deliberately calm down when he or she is excited or all wound up?

   1　2　3　4　5　6　7
   yes　　　　　no

4. Is the quality of the child's work all about the same or does it vary a lot?

   1　2　3　4　5　6　7
   same　　　　varies

5. Does the child work for long-range goals?

   1　2　3　4　5　6　7
   yes　　　　　no

6. When the child asks a question, does he or she wait for an answer, or jump to something else (e.g., a new question) before waiting for an answer?

   1　2　3　4　5　6　7
   waits　　　　jumps

7. Does the child interrupt inappropriately in conversatons with peers, or wait his or her turn to speak?

   1　2　3　4　5　6　7
   waits　　interrupts

8. Does the child stick to what he or she is doing until he or she is finished with it?

   1　2　3　4　5　6　7
   yes　　　　　no

9. Does the child follow the instructions of responsible adults?

   1　2　3　4　5　6　7
   always　　　　never

10. Does the child have to have everything right away?

    1　2　3　4　5　6　7
    yes　　　　　no

11. When the child has to wait in line, does he or she do so patiently?

    1　2　3　4　5　6　7
    yes　　　　　no

12. Does the child sit still?

    1　2　3　4　5　6　7
    yes　　　　　no

13. Can the child follow suggestions of others in group projects, or does he or she insist on imposing his or her own ideas?

    1 2 3 4 5 6 7
    able to   ⎯   imposes
    follow

14. Does the child have to be reminded several times to do something before he or she does it?

    1 2 3 4 5 6 7
    always   ⎯   never

15. When reprimanded, does the child answer back inappropriately?

    1 2 3 4 5 6 7
    always   ⎯   never

From P. C. Kendall and L. E. Wilcox, Self-control in children: Development of a rating scale. *Journal of Consulting and Clinical Psychology,* 1979.

Subject Index

Research, relating learning
  disabilities and emotional
  problems, 15–41

Schizophrenia, childhood, 65–67
Separation anxiety, medications for
  treatment of, 92–93
Separation anxiety disorder, 71–74
  case study, 73–74
  medications for treatment of, 86
Social competence, of learning-
  disabled children, case study,
  46–51
Social problem(s), of children with
  learning disabilities, 3–14

Suicide
  childhood, 70
  depression and, relationship
    between, 70–71

Time-out procedure, in
  management of behavioral
  problems within the
  classroom, 117–118
Tokens, in management of
  behavioral problems within
  the classroom, 118

Vocational training, role of, 124–
  125